I Choose to Laugh

I Choose to Laugh

✦

Faith in the Midst of Cancer

Cara Blakley Smith

with Wallis A. Simpson

iUniverse, Inc.

New York Lincoln Shanghai

I Choose to Laugh
Faith in the Midst of Cancer

iUniverse books may be ordered through booksellers or by contacting:

iUniverse
2021 Pine Lake Road, Suite 100
Lincoln, NE 68512
www.iuniverse.com
1-800-Authors (1-800-288-4677)

Because of the dynamic nature of the Internet, any Web addresses or links contained in this book may have changed since publication and may no longer be valid.

The views expressed in this work are solely those of the author and do not necessarily reflect the views of the publisher, and the publisher hereby disclaims any responsibility for them.

Scripture taken from the Holy Bible, New International Version®. NIV®. Copyright © 1973, 1978, 1984 by International Bible Society. Used by permission of Zondervan Publishing House. All rights reserved.

ISBN: 978-0-595-46623-8 (pbk)
ISBN: 978-0-595-90918-6 (ebk)

Printed in the United States of America

For Larry, Jerry, Gray, and Jim

They will always be my heroes.

Contents

Preface

✦

Why This Book?

I never set out to write a book. I was just supposed to keep people updated on my fifth battle with cancer. Soon my updates became an online journal. I was having conversations with God and others were eavesdropping. Imagine my surprise when a total stranger contacted me. Through two or three degrees of separation, she had been receiving forwards of my updates. She wasn't the only one. By the time God healed me, people were receiving my posts and praying for me in Africa, Australia, Europe, and all across the United States. In May of 2003 when the doctors declared me healed, the online journal stopped. There was nothing left to update.

By mid-summer, I was hearing from my prayer chain. "Have you written anything lately? When are you going to write more? Can't you put it all in a book so I can share it?" So here it is. Every time I backed off from the project, God pushed me forward. He was usually in the guise of my best friend, Wallis Simpson. God's spirit in her never let me give up on this process. She's typed and retyped every word. She's proofed and re-proofed every phrase. She's held my hand through every step. I can never thank her or God enough for her friendship.

My deepest love and thanks, however, goes to my husband, Tim. He knew he was marrying a cancer-scarred woman, and he committed to walk through any valley that might come. Shortly after his promise to love me in sickness and in health, cancer number three came along. With love in his voice and a twinkle in his eye, he turned to me and asked, "Did you come with a warranty?" Yes, I married a man who can laugh. He is my rock, my anchor, and my very best friend. His quiet nature has been my harbor in the storm from the time we met. I love you, Tim, beyond any words I can ever use to express. My love goes to my daughter, Ashley, as well. You are the best thing cancer ever gave me.

Disclaimers

There are two disclaimers I must make. First, I am not a doctor, nurse, technician, or a person with any medical training. This book is not meant to serve as medical advice. Every diagnosis is unique. I cannot stress strongly enough that you must seek out qualified doctors and follow their advice in regard to your condition.

The second is about the title I have chosen. Do not be mistaken. Cancer is no laughing matter, but laughter *is* a life-style choice. It's not so much a chuckle-a-minute-regardless approach. Rather it is choosing to look past the darkness. This book isn't a comedy in the modern sense but more in the Greek drama sense. To the Greeks, a comedy wasn't necessarily funny. It just meant that things ended well for the hero. I like that idea, and I know it's true because to live is Christ and to die is gain. (Philippians 1:21). Life is a divine comedy!

Cara Blakley Smith

E-mail media or speaking engagement requests and/or comments to *ichoosetolaugh@yahoo.com*.

A Note from Wallis

What am I doing here? I stared at the long line of IV bottles, medicines, and worst of all, needles. I was sitting next to my best friend of fourteen years, waiting with her as she received another round of chemotherapy. This was her fifth battle with cancer at the tender age of 35. How could she be so calm? My hands were sweaty, my heart was racing, and the needle wasn't even for me. Fortunately, I could only stay a short while. I had to get to my son's school for another meeting with his teachers. I looked around the room at all the cancer patients and wondered which of us had it the hardest.

My son, Andrew, is a sweet, loving, bright child; not words you would normally use to describe a child with an autism spectrum disorder. My husband and I are blessed. Andrew is intelligent and high functioning, but he is still a tremendous challenge. He keeps us guessing from one day to the next, sometimes one moment to the next, as to what his mood might be. What sound or touch or taste set off the latest temper tantrum? I know it isn't his fault that he doesn't have any self control, but there are days when the patience wears thin and frustration gets the best of me. This was one of those days. Andrew was stuck in a behavioral pattern: not getting any better, not making any progress, and I thought to myself for the hundredth time, "Is this as good as it is going to get?"

Why does there have to be things like cancer and children with special needs? I watched Cara as the nurse tried to insert the needle into her tired veins. She was laughing and joking with the nurse, poke after long poke. If they didn't hurry, I was going to pass out.

When at last the IV was hooked up, I couldn't take it anymore. I blurted out, "I don't get it. How can you be so calm? I could not deal with this. I'm not strong enough to walk this road." Cara thought about it for awhile and answered, "God hasn't asked you to. I can't imagine raising Andrew."

We both realized something that day. We each have our burdens to carry. If God didn't give me cancer, it's because that's not the load He wants me to have. What He gives us often takes us just a step beyond what we can bear by ourselves. That way, we have to give it to Him to carry, and we have to rely on others to encourage and support us.

It has been a privilege to walk this road with Cara. Through her friendship and the process of editing her manuscript, I've seen God in her: in her life, her testimony, and her faith. I've learned that it is possible to laugh at the humor of living. It *is* possible to grow closer to God through the storm, and there *is* purpose in it all, even if we can't see it right now. As Cara has said so often, "If God isn't glorified, it's just a disease!" Our prayer is that this book glorifies God above all else.

Wallis A. Simpson

The Results Are In:
It's Cancer

Dealing with the News

Cancer is cancer. It doesn't matter what kind you are diagnosed with. It's there and you have to deal with it. It will not be ignored. When you feel bad and things seem to go bleak, it's hard to focus on God's love. It's hard to see it clearly when Satan clouds your life with circumstances. If faith is a fact, then you have to arm yourself with facts. There are several things you can do to help make the journey towards healing a little easier.

First, you have to find things worthy of laughter. You have to laugh even when it is an effort. It may be funny movies or a book of jokes. It may be your pets or your best friend. You have to become someone who can see everyday occurrences and find the humor in them. When we get past the fear, the embarrassment, and the pain, life really is funny.

One night after my first surgery, I got the hiccups. I had been out of ICU about two days and was still very sore. You can imagine that the hiccups were excruciatingly painful. Mom was on the phone with Daddy who had called for his nightly check-in. I was eating dinner at the time, which is probably what helped kick off the hiccups.

My youth pastor, John Kramp, had told me once that a sure fire way to cure hiccups was to stick your hand in Jell-O. Of course I can see now that he was just messing with a very gullible middle school girl and I'm sure he got a good chuckle out of it, but that night in the hospital, I didn't know that. All I knew was that the hiccups really hurt, and God had ordained that night's dessert to be green Jell-O.

Yes, I slammed my hand into that Jell-O which started Mom laughing hysterically. I tried to explain why I did it, but I started laughing, too. Daddy was on the other end of the line thinking we had both gone looney, but we had fun. In my pain, with surgical wounds only beginning to heal and radiation treatments looming, we had fun. And do you know what? The hiccups went away. I still think it was the Jell-O that did that.

Second, you make a list that includes those funny things. I call it "The Good List." The good list works like this: Buy a legal pad. Buy a big one, believing that you will fill each page. The bigger the pad, the bigger the faith and the greater the blessing you will receive. Keep the pad next to you at all times. The moment something good happens, write it down. It doesn't matter if it seems small. It's still something. My list included the most seemingly inconsequential things.

I love nature and couldn't see any from the hospital. Once, a bird perched on my window ledge. I put it on the list. I got my favorite flavor of pudding. It went on the list. If I got my favorite nurse or someone sent a sweet card, I put it on the list. I was in the hospital often during my sixteenth year, too sick to leave my hospital bed. My only form of interaction with the world was with whoever entered the room and with the television. Naturally, I got hooked on soap operas. If Bo and Hope got together, I put it on the list.

The key is to spin the negative into a positive so it can go on the list. I had a difficult time keeping in IVs. If I kept one in for 24 hours, I put that on the list. If I only threw up twice instead of four times, it was written down. By the end of the day, the legal pad would be full. Often the list had grown larger than one page.

This list will help you laugh when something bad happens. Basically, you're laughing in the face of Satan because he's going to come back and say, "Here you go. I'm going to make this happen to you today." And you can respond, "Humph, I don't care. That's one thing in my day. You want to see the rest?" You are able to quickly see your blessings. The list of positives gives you a peace because it serves as physical proof that God is taking care of you. Day by day you see His love notes, and it frees you to laugh at something when it comes along.

When you go to bed, keep the list on your nightstand. In the middle of the night, Satan will wake you with whispers of doubt. "God doesn't care. God has abandoned you. God doesn't keep His promises." It will happen, and when it does, reach out in the night and lay your hand on that legal pad. Every line is a love note from God. Every day, all day long, He tells us He loves us. We lose the ability to see it sometimes, but it's there. The minute you focus on your list of positives, Satan will flee.

Lies can't stand up to the truth, and you will have the truth in your hand; black and white, line after line, page after page. Each word is a confirming, victorious shout, "God has not abandoned me! God does care, and He keeps His promises!" And He will continue to whether you write it down or not.

There was one night in the hospital that we couldn't get the air bubbles out of my IV. Granted, they were little air bubbles, but air in your IV line can still be scary. We changed the tubing but still didn't know where they were coming from. Suddenly, we just started laughing. It just became funny to us because we knew God was going to take care of me. We had this list to prove that all day, every day, God was making sure little things were coming along. That day, I was known as "Airhead!" By the time it was all over, we had the nurses laughing with us. If you choose to, you really can laugh at yourself and laugh at the circumstances. When you make that choice, it helps others to find the joy in the moment as well.

It's easy to focus on how bad you feel. But if you can focus on, "Well, I don't feel well today, *but* this good thing happened and this good thing happened …" and the last half of the sentence is positive, it completely changes your outlook. It forces you to focus your attention on the things God is doing for you and not on the things you think He ought to be doing for you but isn't. Be focused on God's plan, not your plan. Make your list, and choose to laugh.

A third thing you need to do is to learn all you can about your disease. The more you know about it, the less fear is involved. The more you can say, "This is what is happening in my body," the less out of control your body seems. The more you do your homework, the more you can talk intelligently with your doctor about what's going on with your body. The more intelligently you speak with your physician, the more you can be comfortable that he knows what he's doing. It also lets your doctor know that you've got a brain, and he doesn't have to baby you with the things that he tells you. He will begin to treat you as an educated member of your treatment team. If you're uncomfortable in any way, you know you need to find a new physician.

There is also a great deal of relief that comes from knowing what is happening and why, even if there isn't anything you can do about it. From the time that we are two years old, we're taught to control our body: use the restroom, don't pass gas or burp, and feed yourself. Now you're in a situation where your body is totally out of your control. The only way that you can get yourself back into what's going on is to know about the disease. Then you control the disease; the disease doesn't control you.

Finally, you have to surround yourself with supportive people. These will be your doctors, nurses, family members, and friends. It is important for these people to be positive and encouraging, trustworthy and honest, helpers and not enablers. There are enough negative circumstances and people. You want to include anyone who will support you through the good days and bad, who will help you to laugh, and who will remind you of the good things life is offering. You can never have too many on your support team.

Like everything else in life, you cannot always choose your circumstances. You can, however, always choose the way you react to them. Cancer, or any other chronic illness, still offers you the choice of how you will handle it. Choose to laugh, to make your list, to know what you are dealing with, and to surround yourself with supportive people. It will make all the difference in your attitude and outlook, and it can make a huge difference in how your life is lived in the long run.

Know Your Rights

It's not uncommon for you to immediately see yourself as a victim as soon as you are diagnosed with cancer. Everything is being done *to* you. Cancer is helping itself to a lovely buffet of your body. Nurses are helping themselves to endless tubes full of your body fluid. Then there are the doctors who can't seem to get enough different types of images. Stand here. Turn this way. Don't eat for 24 hours. Take this. Don't take this. All the while, everyone is suddenly speaking a new language that you have never heard. The most frustrating part is that they seem to be using words that are English, but when you put them all together, they turn into gibberish.

You don't have to be a victim. You can take charge of what is going on. It's your body, your life, and your future. You are your own best advocate, and you need to become an active member of your treatment team. It's not that you can't trust the doctors and what they are telling you, you just need to be a working part of the team.

However, if you feel uncomfortable with your primary oncologist and his team, you need to make some changes. If your doctor can't explain your disease and treatment to you in words you can understand, go find another one. There is no law that says you have to stay with the physician who found your cancer. You want a physician that can kill your cancer. The one who finds it may not be the one to treat it. You've got to work with people with whom you can communicate clearly and who communicate clearly with you.

As soon as you're diagnosed, you are sent into an emotional nosedive. Your mind and emotions are experiencing twists, turns, dips, and rolls that would be the envy of any aerial acrobat. You have a need to get control. The problem is you can't. You can't make your body do anything at this point. The only way you can gain any control is through knowledge.

Your first step must be to find out everything you can about your diagnosis and make sure it's in terms you can comprehend. This book has a small resource section to get you started. These are just a few helpful organizations and websites. It is by no means an exhaustive list. Thanks to the internet, there is a plethora of information at your fingertips. It's important to not overwhelm yourself with too much information. Just begin to learn to speak the jargon.

Make your doctor explain everything to you slowly, clearly, and with lots of opportunities for you to ask questions. It's your body, and you have every right to know exactly what's going on. You can't change what has happened, but knowing what may come next can give you some power. The more you know, the fewer surprises there are. If you are discussing your disease with your doctor on a regular basis and bringing educated questions to him, when your treatment changes or your body changes, you are prepared.

The unknown is frightening. I've found in talking to people that the scariest time with cancer for most people seems to be the period between the "I may have something," and "The name for what I have is____, and we are going to do ____ about it." We cannot change the diagnosis, but we can learn what it means and how it will affect us, our families, and our lives. We learn what to expect and when to expect it. From here on out, the unpredictable is the norm. The more you can anticipate what may come, the less fear there is when it happens. Knowledge is power and in the fight against cancer, you need all the power you can get. The question is how do you gain the knowledge?

First, do your research. Look on the internet, read books, and ask your doctors and nurses lots of questions. The second thing is very important. Invest in a three-ring binder and a set of tabbed dividers. The notebook is to keep every report you get, every website from which you print information, every question you ask, and the answers you receive. I recommend dividing the notebook into the following sections: lab/test results, research information, treatment/medication log (this should include all of your medications and their side effects information), questions to ask the doctor (have blank paper for note taking), and insurance/billing information. Put a date on every piece of paper.

Always keep your notebook on hand. You will think of questions at 2:00am. Write them down. Then when you go to the doctor, you have it with you. This is so important because chemo destroys your memory skills. Be sure to take the notebook with you to every appointment.

Take notes! You might even want to invest in a digital voice recorder so you don't miss anything. So much information comes flying at you in such a short time. Do everything you can to retain it. I also recommend that you never go to an appointment alone. A second set of ears is invaluable. They might think of questions to ask that never occurred to you or be aware of something you haven't noticed.

Case in point: I took my daughter to a check-up one day. Doctors usually have a long questionnaire that you always fill out. It assesses the current physical and emotional side effects and helps them know what the focus of your visit may need to be. Ashley was helping me fill it out. When the question came up about hearing loss, I skipped it. Ashley stopped me and said, "But Momma, you do have trouble hearing now. You always have to ask me to speak up, and in the car I have to be loud and repeat things." I hadn't thought about it, but it was true. My doctor and I discussed it and addressed the issue. It turns out hearing loss can be a side effect of certain chemo treatments. If I hadn't had my daughter with me, it wouldn't have even come up.

The bottom line is this, don't let your doctor out of your exam room until you are fully satisfied that you understand what's happening as much as possible. Don't say things like, "Well, he's a busy man," or "I don't want to trouble him with little things." Bar the door and stand your ground. It may be a new experience for you to be assertive, especially with an educated professional, but don't back down. It's your body. It's your life. He or she is there to treat you. Don't be afraid to be selfish in a positive sense. Know your rights and act within them. Do it as if your life depends on it because it just might.

Questions to Ask

There is so much you want to know, it's hard to know where to begin. You want to know everything. Still, it can be scary and overwhelming. Where do you start? Here's a list of things that I felt were critical for me to know. It isn't comprehensive. It's just to get you thinking. Remember there is no such thing as a stupid question. You don't have a medical degree. Well, maybe some of you do. I sure didn't, but that's no reason why I couldn't understand what was being done to me and for me. Never hesitate to ask for clarification.

What is my diagnosis? Get a specific name.

What is my prognosis? Understand this is often difficult to determine so you may not really get a solid answer. Prognosis is a process and sometimes something as simple as a positive attitude and a will to live can impact it.

What needs to be our immediate course of action?

What are all the treatment options? Do your research on this one. Know them yourself, and then ask your doctor. Ask why he has chosen a certain plan for you as opposed to other options.

How long of a process will the treatment be? Find out if they are talking days (thyroid cancer treatments are sometimes only three days long), months, or years. If it involves surgery, what will be the hospitalization and recovery time?

What are your (the physician's) expectations and goals for my treatment? Are we expecting complete eradication of the disease, remission, or the slowing of metastasis?

What is going to be normal for me now?

Will I see a change in my energy level and if so, how soon?

Do I need to limit my activities and contact with people, or can I keep doing what I want as long as I feel I have the energy for it?

How is my life going to be different when I am finished with everything? What, if any, lifetime changes will I need to make?

What are <u>all</u> the possible side effects of what I am taking? I stress the word "all" because there's always this tiny percentage of people that have extreme reactions. My family and I have learned to always ask about the rarest and most extreme things to expect because it is a sure fire guarantee that my body will go there. It's become a joke to us. My most recent oncologist didn't take me completely seriously about this. All it took was one treatment, and my body went haywire. It made a believer out of him in a hurry. Keep in mind, most people are not going to respond violently or strongly, but it's better to know all the possibilities. That way if something does happen, you know why and what to do.

Will I lose my hair? Sometimes they can tell you down to within a two to three day period so you can really plan. They told me I would lose mine between days 14 and 17 after my first treatment. I scheduled a photo session for day 10 for one last day of glory. On day 15 I took a shower and as I washed my hair, most of it came out by the handfuls.

How do we handle insurance and payments?

If I don't feel "right," what should I do?

What emergency room should I use, and what special instructions should I give them when I arrive? Many emergency rooms will immediately isolate chemo patients because they understand that you have a weakened immune system and are in a very susceptible state to all the disease floating in the waiting room.

Obtain a copy of the hospital and doctor's office patient rights material, and familiarize yourself with them.

Overall, you need to understand that your primary job for the next however many months it takes is to be completely self-centered. Don't worry about hurting your doctor's feelings. Don't worry about inconveniencing a nurse. Don't worry about pestering a receptionist. Granted, you need to be patient and polite, but don't hesitate to cut loose and make demands if you are not being cared for in the proper manner.

For example, my Hodgkin's disease treatments at sixteen were very debilitating to my immune system, and I spent most of my time in the hospital. It almost became a routine: take a treatment, wait five days, watch my fever climb quickly, start to feel really bad, be admitted to the hospital. During one of these cycles I was sitting in the waiting room of the admitting office of the hospital. We had been at the doctor's office where I was as comfortable as I could be for the time being. The hospital admitting office had told us to wait there. They would call over when a room was ready so I could go straight to my room. When we got the call and showed up, a room was not ready. I was left to wait for over an hour, sitting in a wheelchair in a very public waiting room, shivering with a very high fever. I remember asking for a blanket because I was so cold from my fever chills. Mom asked a receptionist who told her there were no blankets.

It was the last straw. My mother proceeded to walk across the hall to a physical therapy room where she politely obtained a blanket for me. She then very clearly insisted that the admissions supervisor be summoned immediately. Mom proceeded to assertively raise some dust. When the cloud had settled, the hospital had apologized, I was quickly in a room, and the admission's office had a permanent stash of blankets on hand. The bottom line is that the hospital and any medical staff are there to meet your needs. Make sure they do, and don't be shy about it. Ask questions, and insist on clear answers. It's your health and your life. Fight for it. If you don't, no one will.

When Cancer Comes Back

Again. It's usually a good word. "Can I see you again?" "When are you going to fix that delicious dessert again?" "That roller coaster was incredible! Let's ride it again!" *Again.* It speaks of repeated pleasures and second chances, until you hear it in your oncologist's office. Suddenly it takes on the context of a certain death sentence. I beat cancer only to get it ... again.

I have personally experienced that phrase four times. For those who are mathematically challenged like me, that means I've had cancer five times. It wasn't always the same kind. I'm an equal opportunity cancer kind of gal. I had Hodgkin's disease (lymphatic cancer) twice in my teens. I had thyroid cancer twice in my twenties. I had breast cancer once in my thirties. It seems I'm finally slowly weaning myself off my cancer habit, and I'm hoping to be able to quit cold turkey in my 40s. All joking aside, I know intimately what it means to hear the word "again."

It's not an easy word to hear. Somehow we get this idea in our heads that if we can beat cancer we can beat anything, and it will never come back for us. I suppose I lived on the old lightning-can't-strike-in-the-same-place-twice philosophy. Apparently it's true. It doesn't strike twice. It goes for broke. Each time I was diagnosed "again," I had a different reaction, a different range of emotion.

After my first cancer, I lived in fear for three years that it might come back. What would I do? How would I continue my life? I was 13, 14 and 15 years old. My teenage universe was obviously revolving around me, and the future was hard, if not impossible, to conceive. Somehow when I received the word that my Hodgkin's disease had returned, it was almost a relief. Yes, the worst had happened, but at least I wasn't looking over my shoulder waiting for it to catch up with me anymore. The worst had happened, and I was still alive. There was still hope, and life was still going to go on.

It was a huge lesson to learn at 15 but one I immediately recognized and appreciated. God knew I would never get on with life until I let go of the fear of not getting to live it. That anxiety had paralyzed me emotionally. It was as if I was stuck on a ladder high above the ground, too afraid to move up or down, just hanging on for dear life. That second diagnosis got me going again, and I made a decision. From that moment on I would live, regardless of whether or not I might die. Essentially I had turned myself into that little old cat lady who's afraid to come out of her house for fear she might get hit by a car or bus or some other random incident. We all laugh at her, and yet I had become her.

The third time I was diagnosed with cancer I was caught completely by surprise. I guess I thought it was kind of like getting the chicken pox. Once you beat it, you were immune to it forever. Unfortunately, that isn't the case. For me, it was most likely the treatment for my Hodgkin's disease that created the opportunity for my papillary thyroid cancer. During my first round of Hodgkin's I received radiation treatment. The mantel, or treatment area, included my neck so my thyroid received massive doses of radiation which was an invitation for the cells to mutate and take over my body. True to form, my system rose to the occasion. It wasn't as scary as it had been the second time. I'd been at "again" once before and come out the other side so I didn't have a sense of hopelessness or despair. It was more just resignation and impatience. *Okay, okay, I have cancer again. Let's deal with it and move on. I have a life to live.*

Fortunately for me, thyroid cancer is very simply and effectively treated with a dose of radioactive iodine. I also opted for surgery to be safe. My thyroid had not been working correctly for several years. Losing it could be compensated for with medication. My thought was to get out everything with the potential to be bad and move on. It worked great for three years. Then in May of 1997, just days before my first Mother's Day and my thirtieth birthday, I went in for a check-up.

By now, I have developed a Pavlovian response to check-ups. I almost expect to get bad news. On that date, however, I really wasn't expecting anything; just an evaluation of my thyroid replacement medication dosage, a pat on the head, and see you later. Hearing "again" for the third time in my life sent me into a panic. Total fear seized me. Now it just wasn't my life, it was the life of my new baby girl. I had to be a mother. I couldn't have cancer.

I excused myself to the bathroom where I proceeded to completely fall apart like I never had before. I found myself curled into a fetal ball in the corner, searching my mind desperately for an answer or at least some comfort. God, being God, did not disappoint me. He also didn't fail to give me a point of laughter in the midst of the fear. Sitting there with my whirling emotions, fears, and questions, I could only crystallize one coherent thought. It was the chorus of a *Veggie Tales* song: "God is bigger than the boogie man. He's bigger than Godzilla or the monsters on TV. Oh, God is bigger than the boogie man, and He's watching out for you and me."[1] I had watched it many times with my daughter, and God had stored the truth in my heart for just that moment.

So there I was, sitting on the tile floor of a doctor's office bathroom with tears and snot running everywhere, and I'm laughing and singing out loud. I'm sure it was an interesting sight, and I felt certain the arrival of the men in white coats was imminent. But the reality I learned that day was God *is* bigger than the boogie man. God is bigger than my fear. God is bigger than any cancer, and God absolutely loves "again."

The hardest "again" was definitely the latest one; breast cancer. I pray it's the last one. Up to this point I'd had the easy cancers. Lymphatic cancers tend to have a very good treatment result. Thyroid cancer is quickly dealt with and hardly even interrupts your life. Breast cancer kills people. At least that was the message in my head. I felt like Red Foxx on *Sanford and Son*: this is the big one. This is the one that is going to kill me. You can push your luck only so far, right? My solution? Deny it was happening.

Denial is easy enough. If I don't admit to myself emotionally that "again" has happened yet again then it hasn't happened. I taught myself within a matter of moments to be able to speak facts and totally disassociate myself from what they meant. I appeared calm, collected, and quite brave, quite the contrast from the previous time. I was so proud of myself, so strong for everyone around me. My mind had totally shut out the truth and refused to open the door to it.

I was diagnosed in December after my first mammogram. What no one had told me was that Hodgkin's disease had put me at a very high risk for breast cancer. I was pretty much sure to contract it at some point. We met with the oncologist, scheduled the surgeries, discussed the things that needed to be discussed, and I was as cool as a cucumber, never a tear shed and never a quiver in my voice.

It was a day or two before my surgery. I was spending time with my best friend just sitting and chatting when it all fell apart. She asked me how I was *really* doing. I looked at her to give the appropriate, programmed response. I opened my mouth to utter the well-rehearsed "I'm fine," and nothing came out. I remember literally choking and tasting the rising gorge in my throat. Suddenly, the wall was down. The door flew open and every black, dark, ugly thought, fear, and emotion rushed in. It wasn't pretty. I was so mad at God; dare I say furious? *God, my testimony is beefed up enough. Find somebody else to do your dirty work. I'm tired of You picking on me!* Amazingly enough, the house was not struck with lightning. God permitted me to rant, and rant I did. I'm not sure how long it went on. I just remember when the tirade of fury was over, I was a cried out,

---

1.   ©BOB AND LARRY PUBLISHING (EMI CHRISTIAN MUSIC)/NEW SPRING, INC./SVT SONGS. All Rights Reserved. Used By Permission.

exhausted shell collapsed on the bed. My best friend just sat there stroking my hair. I'm not sure she ever said a word.

People ask me, "What do you do if it comes back?" I can't tell you how you'll respond. I can only tell you where I landed after I went through each of my varied responses. After the first "again," I made a decision to trust God. It was a decision made void of emotion because obviously emotions will change. Rather it was based on fact, and it was my anchor for every "again" I encountered. God loves me. God has a plan for my life. God is bigger than me, and I feel fairly confident that He knows what He's doing, even if I do feel the need to question it from time to time. So I'll let God be God. I'll let Him design the plan, and I'll just go with it.

There's a lot of peace that comes in knowing it's not my responsibly to know why or even how. I just need to know one thing; God. If it wasn't cancer, God would put something else in my life to bring me to Him. For some reason, I was just designed for this. The key thing I come back to after the fear, denial, and anger is that God knows what He's doing and "again" never catches Him by surprise. As unexpected and unwelcome as cancer might have been in my life, He was planning and preparing for it all along. *Gee, thanks God. Couldn't we plan more trips to Hawaii and fewer trips to the hospital?* Apparently that's not in my agenda. Oh, well.

Sometimes I wonder if there are more "agains" for me. What if it comes back? Can we beat it another time? Will it be a variation of a past cancer or something new altogether? I was at extremely high risk for ovarian and cervical cancer so we took care of that before it could get any sassy ideas about mutating on me. With my weird body, I might just create a whole new specimen of cancer no one has seen before. Hey, everybody needs to be an achiever at something. The bottom line is, "again" or no "again," I just have to keep living my life. The moment I stop living my life, I'm dead, and I'm not ready to be that just yet if you know what I mean.

Chemotherapy's
Physical Effects

Prepare Yourself

Chemotherapy: The gift that keeps on giving. Some people already feel pretty bad by the time a chemo regimen is settled on. Me, I felt fine. If it weren't for those high tech pictures, it would have been hard to believe I was as sick as I was. Chemo was the wake-up call for me. The cancer didn't make me feel sick, but chemo took me for a rough ride. In order to understand why it can be so devastating to your system, you need to understand how it works and how to prepare yourself.

Simply put, chemotherapy is an orchestrated, planned, coordinated, poisonous attack on anything in your system that reproduces quickly. This explains why so many different systems in your body suffer. You suffer nausea because your gastric system and digestive system are disrupted. They work quickly. Your white blood cells reproduce and grow quickly, so your ability to fight infection disappears. Your energy level drops because the production of red blood cells that carry oxygen to your system is slowed down. Hair grows quickly, so it's gone. On a side note, when hair growth stops, *all* hair growth stops; that includes legs and armpits, ladies. That may be chemo's bright side.

Over the years, chemotherapy has been refined to attack only certain types of cells, so it's not an attack on your entire system. Even so, it's not like swallowing your dose of nasty castor oil and getting on with your life. Chemo will bring on a life change. Still, chemo doesn't have to have complete control over how you live your life. You just need to be aware of what will probably happen and make plans.

The biggest change chemo brought about in my life dealt with my energy level. The more treatments I received, the more tired I became. Granted, some of that was emotional, but overall chemo just makes you tired. This means you need to plan ahead. Cut back on the things that you don't really need to be spending your time on. Know that your energy will be limited and choose to spend it wisely. I got to the point where I planned activities around when my treatments would occur because I could predict when my stamina would play out. I usually felt my best the day or two before my next treatment so I would plan outings for those days.

I would also plan shorter outings than I usually took. Don't do the shopping mall, the grocery store, and the veterinarian all in the same day. If you actually make it through it all without needing a wheelchair, you'll pay for it the next day. This was a big thing for me to learn. I'm a go, go, go kind of girl and slowing down was next to impossible. I almost felt like I had failed because I couldn't keep up with my regular schedule. I had to look at myself in the mirror on a regular basis and remind myself, "Honey, you've got cancer. You can't go gangbusters anymore. There's no shame in it. Just pick one thing and enjoy it. Save the rest for another day." Good advice. It just took me forever to follow it.

Another change you will face is your system's ability to fight infection. Your white blood cells are the things in your blood that attack any foreign invader, from a cold to major diseases. Chemo makes it hard for this little soldier to do his job. Consequently, it is much easier for you to get sick and getting sick is much more dangerous.

The chemotherapy I received for my Hodgkin's disease in the early 1980's just about killed me. I was in the hospital an average of two weeks every month for six months. Why? Infections. Someone else's common cold can knock a cancer patient into a 104 degree fever and an extended hospital stay on the immuno-suppression ward. You have to train your family and friends to be careful around you if they have the sniffles or a cough. Wash your hands often, especially if you are around children on a regular basis. Most importantly, learn what your base or average temperature is and never take it lightly when it goes up a few degrees. Call your doctor immediately if your temperature starts to go up, and don't hesitate to head to the emergency room.

If you do go to the ER or a doctor's office, let them know right away that your immune system is not working at full capacity. A good ER will immediately isolate you from other patients in the waiting room so as not to make the problem worse. There are many new drugs available now to combat the problem of a suppressed immune system, and they are truly amazing. They even have some to help with energy. Be sure to ask your doctor about them. Drugs like Neulasta® can really have an impact on your quality of life during treatment.

One final thing you need to prepare yourself for is something no one warned me about. Now, it doesn't happen to everyone, but most people I've talked to have experienced it to some degree. I'm talking about sleep patterns. Something about chemo really messes with your sleeping habits. You might find that you want to sleep all the time. Other people experience insomnia. My problem was that I turned into a vampire. Okay, not really, but I sure got my days and nights reversed. What happened is that I would feel really tired because I didn't sleep well so I would take a nap. Then I wouldn't be sleepy again until late. I wouldn't sleep well so I would be even more tired the next day, and the nap would be even longer. Of course, that meant I wouldn't be able to go to sleep until even later, and before I knew it, I was intimately familiar with all the late night television programming.

It's important to rest when you are tired, but try to keep your days as days and your nights as nights. The body heals as it sleeps, and you will be more tired than you have ever been before, but it's still important to try to keep to a normal schedule as much as possible. Don't hesitate to talk to your doctor about any problems you have with sleeping.

No one should ever make light of the effects chemotherapy has on a person's body. It can be devastating. Denial won't make it go away. Share the effects with others so they can understand and be helpful. Talk to your doctor about any concerns. Remember, solid knowledge and good preparation can help to minimize the control chemo has over your life.

Count Your Losses

Cancer and chemotherapy are traumatic to your body. You'll never be the same again. One of the difficult things for me about chemo was trying to figure out what "normal" was and then learning that I would have to redefine "normal" for the rest of my life. The tricky part is that I've never been normal to start with; just ask my friends and family. Now I have an excuse! Who wouldn't love to spend the rest of their life with that easy excuse for odd behavior? "Sorry, it's not me. It's the chemo."

Seriously, "normal" and "well" take on a new definition because chemo leaves you different than it found you. Primarily for me, the key issue was diminished brain capacity. By that I mean that during and after my chemotherapy, I had a significant disability. I found it almost impossible to concentrate on things, to maintain my focus. My short term memory was gone, and my long term memory seemed impaired. Multi-task? I was doing well if I could use words with multiple syllables.

I started teaching high school three months after my breast cancer treatments. I immediately explained to my students about "chemo days" and "chemo brain." It goes like this. Chemo gave me brain damage in that my brain doesn't work like it used to. My parents talk about getting older and how their minds seem to be slipping. I was there at 35. As the chemo gradually left my system, my mental capacities returned, but even today I notice that I'm not as sharp as I used to be. When I have one of my special moments when my mind completely shuts down, my loving husband likes to remind me that I'm brain damaged. I usually smile and reply, "Yes, dear, I know. But what is your excuse?"

Having my mind move directly into advanced senior adult status is not the only change I experienced as a result of chemotherapy. At the age of 16 I entered menopause. My chemo for Hodgkin's disease destroyed all my eggs which left me unable to conceive or bear children. That was a loss I struggled with for years. Then God allowed us to adopt our daughter, and I can't be more thankful that I could never have children of "my own." My daughter is the sunshine of my life, and if I hadn't had cancer and extreme chemotherapy, someone else would be raising her right now. Still, at the time I didn't know my precious child was coming, and no one realized what my body was doing as a result of chemo. I was going through menopause and puberty at the same time. You want to talk about a crazy ride! I was bouncing from one emotional state to the next, usually only a minute or two apart.

At the age of 35, after two rounds of chemo and three rounds of radiation treatments, I was unable to think clearly like I felt I should, was way beyond menopause, and was losing my hearing. Oh, yes, my hearing was going thanks to the latest round of chemo. I didn't even know that was a possibility. Apparently it's pretty rare, but you have to be prepared for the unusual.

Take for instance, post-breast cancer. When lymph nodes are removed from your armpit, the potential for a condition called lymphodemia arises. This is where your arm will retain fluid and can swell up to many times its original size. It seems you can't work the arm in question too much because that is what causes the fluid retention.

I'm also more easily tired out than ever before. Even though I finished my last round of chemo several years ago, I still find that I have to pick and choose how I will expend my energy. I just don't have as much to go around as I used to. I also have to be very careful about being around people who are contagious. With all that my body has been through, it just doesn't fight off illness like it should. I have learned to slow down more, slow down sooner, and give myself longer to get well if I do get sick. That has been really hard for me because other people my age don't deal with this, and I compare myself to them. I'm always afraid that people will think I'm lazy or slacking off because I can't keep up with the pace. It's also hard because I don't want to miss out on anything.

It's nice to know why I'm a lap behind everyone else, but it doesn't change the fact that I'd rather be in the lead. Dealing with the various losses takes time, but at least I'm still running the race. I guess if I look at it that way, I really don't have anything to complain about.

Where Your Mouth Is

Think of your favorite food: Grandma's cherry cobbler, hot fries fresh from the fryer, chocolate. Now imagine that it tastes like cardboard and even worse, it hurts to chew or swallow it. Even if you do get it down, most likely it won't stay down. That's what chemo will do for you. Chemo affects every part of your body including your mouth. It's one of the things you don't hear about much, but it is just as common as hair loss and fatigue.

The easiest "eating" side effect to understand is nausea. If you understand that chemo is attacking everything in your system that reproduces quickly then it only stands to reason that your gastric juices will be affected. Fortunately there are many anti-nausea medicines available today that weren't around 20 years ago.

The first time I had chemo was in the 1980's. I was sick all the time so I was surprised in 2003 when I had chemo again that I didn't get sick nearly as much as I had expected. Be sure to ask your doctor to prescribe something for nausea up front. Even if you aren't having a problem at first, it saves time and misery if you already have something on hand when the situation arises, if you know what I mean.

Even if you aren't having trouble keeping your food down, cancer treatment can really change your eating habits. Most people find that they see a significant loss in appetite. That's the way it usually seems to be with the human body. You get sick, and you don't want to eat. However, sometimes the opposite is true.

It's not uncommon for different types of steroids to be part of a chemotherapy regimen. I've been told it helps to counteract the extreme side effects. As a teenage girl, being on steroids was both interesting and an embarrassment to my family. I lost weight rapidly from the chemo, but the steroids made me so hungry, I out-ate the football players. We would go out with friends, and I would clean my plate and everyone else's. Even though I ate like a linebacker, the pounds dropped off at an alarming rate.

When I was diagnosed with breast cancer and was looking for anything positive, I remembered the remarkable weight loss from Hodgkin's disease. I thought I had found a bright spot in my ordeal. By the age of 35 I had managed to gain a little more padding in my hips and torso than I wanted or needed. Let's just say I was a little "fluffy." I decided to look at this new round of chemo as an extreme diet plan. Yes, I'd be sick and tired for several months, but just think how thin I'd be when it was all over!

Imagine my surprise when I started gaining pounds and inches. I mentioned it to my doctor, and he explained that several types of treatments actually cause you to gain weight. I didn't appreciate him not being on board with my extreme make-over plan and semi-jokingly asked if we could switch me over the one of the "lose pounds" treatments. It doesn't work that way, but he got a good laugh out of it.

Another big problem for many chemo patients is mouth sores. These are not so much like little ulcers. These are more like when you scald your tongue, and it feels raw, only it's all over the tongue and walls of the mouth. I can't explain all the reasons why they are so prevalent. All I know is that they hurt, and even if you're hungry and are able to eat, it hurts to swallow even a milk shake. I've learned some tricks to keeping the mouth sores from being as bad as they could be.

First, take hard candy with you to your treatment. Suck on the candy and crushed ice during the entire drip. There is something about keeping the saliva flowing through the mouth that keeps the toxins from settling there as much, even though it may not keep the sores away. Second, try chewing spearmint or peppermint gum. When I did, the coolness of the flavor seemed to soothe my mouth.

Third, I learned how to turn everything into a milkshake so I wouldn't have to chew. Sonic® became my new best friend. Finally, there are medicines that you can ask for to help with the pain. These are usually gels and sprays for the inside of your mouth.

The worst part for my mouth was how chemo changed the taste of food. None of my favorite foods tasted right. They didn't necessarily taste bad, they just didn't taste right. I'm sure the ladies will understand what I mean when I say I depend on chocolate. I was so sad that I lost the taste of it during my treatments.

Fortunately this is only a short term thing. My taste buds returned to normal as the last of the toxins left my body. I don't know what I would have done if I had lost the taste of chocolate forever. As I looked for a silver lining, I thought that maybe if my favorite food tasted worse, then my least favorite foods would taste better. No such luck. Not even extreme chemo can change the taste of boiled turnip greens.

It's important to keep in mind that you must continue eating regardless of any side-effects you may be battling. Your body is fighting a war and needs constant re-enforcements. There are many foods that naturally fight cancer and can help counteract side-effects. Ask your doctor or a nutritionist for information. Find out *how* you should eat and *what* you should eat, but the main thing is that you keep eating. Once the chemo leaves your body, you should find the various effects on your mouth dissipate and then it's bon appétit!

Hair Loss Is for the Birds

One thing most people will face when going through chemotherapy is hair loss: not just on your head but all over your body. This can be a good thing if you don't like to shave. However, it can be a real shock the first time you run your fingers through your hair and it sticks to your hand. Suddenly, hair is everywhere.

One day, I stood in the back yard, shedding like a collie and thinking about myself and my hair loss. As I watched my beautiful locks float away on the breeze, I heard my mother-in-law exclaim, "Oh, the birds will love this!" I turned to see her holding a fist full of my discarded hair and running to place it beneath the bird houses she has in her yard. "Do you have anymore?" she asked. Well, yeah, as a matter of fact. I still have a lot.

That's when it hit me. There's a passage in the Bible about how God takes care of the birds of the air. I always assumed that was God's way of telling me that He would take care of me; a metaphor. That day, I heard Him quietly say to me, "No, I really meant the birds. Your hair is terrific for their nests. I don't waste the things I make. Every thing, absolutely every thing, has a purpose in my plan. Even the hair on your head has a purpose which, by the way, I still know the number even though it's changing by the second."

Yes, I was humbled. Just because God loves me doesn't mean the rest of His creation is less precious to Him. He loves those birds, too. Then I heard Him finish. "That passage was meant for you, too. I love you more than the birds, My child. And if I care enough to make sure the birds have nice, soft hair for their nests, I care enough to make sure your head is taken care of as well." At that moment I came to a decision. I was going to shave off the rest of my hair and place it next to the birdbath.

It's funny to me that with all the other things I was facing, the hardest thing for me was to cut my hair. I began wearing a hat everywhere so I wouldn't leave a trail of shed hairs. Sleeping in a knit toboggan cap kept it off my pillow. There isn't much help for the shower drain until it's all gone. As depressing as it was to see the hair coming out in clumps, it was hard to give the go-ahead to just shave it all.

A word of warning: don't decide to get rid of all your hair the same day the last cold front of winter blows through town! When it was all said and done, the hairdresser thought I had a nicely shaped head. You're never sure about that until you can see it all. As I walked out of the beauty shop, I saw that a lady was staring at me. It made me laugh. I just looked at her and smiled and said, "Breast cancer." She got this look of pity on her face and said, "I'm so sorry." I wasn't sorry, though. It gave me more opportunities to share about Jesus and how He was taking care of me.

Once the hair is gone, whether through natural causes or shaving it, the cool thing is to rub your head. It feels so strange! The first thing my daughter said when she saw me bald was, "Mommy, aren't you afraid people will laugh at you?" This is a legitimate concern. It is difficult to look in the mirror the first few times. But the truth is you are more than your hair. God made you special, and it doesn't matter what other people think as long as you know God thinks you are wonderful.

There are a few things that no one bothers to tell you about when you lose your hair; questions you thought you'd never ask and pieces of information you never thought you'd need. For example, when in the sun, be sure to apply sunscreen to your newly revealed scalp. It's never seen the sun before. I guess some men have learned this lesson, but there are no helpful posters plastering the walls of the wig shops for women.

Did you know your head sweats? Well, sure, when you think about it, it makes sense. That's how our hair gets dirty, right? Well, without hair, all that sweat just runs down your face, so I came up with a solution. My husband and I used to have two sisters in our youth group who played in the school marching band. Allison and Abby hated wearing socks so they just covered their feet with anti-perspirant before putting on their shoes. It seemed to work for them.

I took the same principle and applied it to my head, literally. Of course, there was some trial and error work finding out which anti-perspirants leave a residue and which dry the fastest. I recommend the clear gels. They apply the easiest and don't look scaly when they dry. Laugh all you want, but my head didn't drip once all summer, and I never had sweat in my eyes. Hey, I may have to be bald, but I can still do it with style. We just have to figure these things out for ourselves.

Remember being told as a kid that you lose a lot of body heat through your head? You'd be amazed how cold it can be at night without hair. I invested in a very soft, non-wool, non-itchy stocking cap to keep the chill out.

The one question no one could ever answer for me remains a mystery. I have sold several different brands of make-up during my life. They all teach you to apply your foundation to the hair line. Do you see where I'm going with this one? I didn't have a hairline. So where does the make-up stop? Do I just keep blending all the way to the back of my neck? I opted for leaving the foundation out of my cosmetic regimen. It just seemed simpler.

Overall, hair loss had its advantages. I'm a low maintenance girl, and you just can't get any easier than never having a bad hair day because you don't have any hair. My family was jealous that I could climb right out of the pool and be instantly ready for Sunday evening church.

Since my last round of chemo, I've been growing hair like crazy. I haven't cut it in four years. *Locks for Love* is one of several charities that receive donations of cut hair. They will turn that hair into a wig and pass it on to a child currently undergoing cancer treatments. You can call or visit their website for the specifics of donating. So, I'm farming hair for them. I'll grow this crop until I've got at least 12 inches. I'd like to be able to donate 20 inches because I remember how important having long hair was to me. As soon as I cut it and donate it, I'll start on another crop. My daughter is even farming with me.

It's good to know that someday, the hair will come back. You may get a new style you've never had before. Chances are you'll never take it for granted again. Every time I brush my hair it just reminds me that everything I have is a gift from God, and everything He gives me I'm to use to glorify Him in some way. God gave me hair. God took my hair away. God gave me hair again. God took my hair again. God gave me hair again. Now it's my turn to give it away for God. Hairs to God!

Meet My Wigs:
Frieda and Bridgette

One of the hard things about cancer is the way it changes how you see yourself. You no longer look in the mirror and see a healthy person. Your self image is radically altered by the impact of steroids, diet changes, and fatigue, not to mention what all those chemicals do to your complexion. If you are someone who draws your self worth from how you look, you're going to have to find a new foundation for your value. But wigs are a wonderful tool to help in the transition. They can give you confidence and laughter. Just ask Frieda and Bridgette.

Losing your hair can be hard. There's just something not right about it coming out by the handfuls as if you were a Persian cat in summer. It wasn't so bad for me the second time I lost my hair. I had been through it before and didn't care what people thought. But the first time, I was 16 and cared a great deal.

We are bombarded daily with messages that how you look is everything, and if you don't look good, you aren't good. This was not good news when the only physical feature I felt I had going for me was my long, dark hair. I'd finally gotten it to style the way I wanted, and for the first time I was beginning to feel as if I could look just like everybody else; I could fit in.

Well, I guess God felt the need to drive home to me that He created me to be an individual. Just a few weeks after chemo began I was shedding more than my mohair sweater. I couldn't bring myself to cut my hair, which came past my shoulders, so hair was everywhere. My family was gracious enough to understand how important my hair was to me and never said a word. Within a month, however, it became apparent that I was either going to have to go public with my baldness or invest in a wig.

My mother tried to be helpful. She went and picked out a wig for me. Now, while it's great to want to help and all, hair is a very personal thing. What I thought looked good on me and what Mom considered "cute" were two totally different looks. Word to the reader here, if you want to help, offer to drive, accompany or even pay. But don't go and pick out a wig on your own and spring it on the patient. Needless to say, it was a little traumatic.

I was in the hospital when Mom brought it to the room with such pride. The thought of a wig was hard for me to accept. When I saw it, it was all I could do not to laugh and cry at the same time. It looked like something my grandmother would wear. It may have been sophisticated and cute, but it certainly wasn't how I saw myself.

I wouldn't have believed it at the time, but wigs can provide great moments of humor. Not long after my mother bought the wig, I asked my boyfriend to run his fingers through what was left of my hair. He walked straight over to the wig sitting on its white Styrofoam head and started to pet it. I was so mad but then I had to laugh. I named the wig Frieda. No offense to all the Friedas out there. It was a nice wig. It just wasn't a "Cara." For Christmas I was allowed to pick out another wig more to my liking, and I named it Bridgette.

On one particular day, I was out with a bunch of friends from church at a pizza parlor. I was wearing Bridgette. The restaurant began to play "Dixie" which was our school fight song. My friend, Raleigh, stood up and shouted, "They're playing our song! Show your respect!" I immediately stood up, ripped Bridgette from my bald pate, and held her over my heart as any red-blooded American with a head covering would do during the national anthem or school fight song as the case may be. People were spewing drinks and choking on pizza over that one.

I learned something that day. It's important to be able to laugh about what's happening to you, but you also have to teach people around you how to laugh about it too. You have to let them know that it's okay to chuckle about how ridiculous the whole situation can seem sometimes.

Another time, I was on a choir mission trip to Houston, Texas, which is perhaps the most humid spot on the entire planet. My roommates would get up two hours early to put their hair in hot rollers. (This was when big hair was the style.) They would brush, tease, and spray their hair only to have it completely collapse the moment we stepped out of the hotel. I would get up 30 minutes before we had to leave. I'd brush my teeth, apply a little make-up, shake out my wig and go on my merry way. My hair was perfect all day long. For once my hair, which wasn't even really hair at all much less mine, was the envy of every girl I met. I guess it's all a matter of perspective.

Chemotherapy's
Emotional Effects

Facing Your Mortality

Being diagnosed with cancer as a teenager has some unique challenges to it. Let's face it. Teenagers live in a different world than adults. They are possessed with an amazing mythology that they are indestructible, the whole world lies ahead of them, and nothing stands in their way of total success. The jaded adult refers to it as naiveté, but I prefer to see it as boundless optimism and a heart not yet tainted with some of the harsh realities of life. A problem with this mythology arises when it is directly challenged. It can be a problem for anyone at any age, really.

In 1983, in my personal vocabulary, cancer was synonymous with death. We were an uneducated student culture. AIDS didn't even come on the scene until I was in college. We were very medically unaware. Most people didn't even know how you contracted cancer, and we had heard so little about people surviving it. I've worked with teenagers since my driver's license says I stopped being one, and I know one thing is certain, if you challenge their mythology, they will shut you out. Because of this defense mechanism, on a large part, I was shut out as well.

It's hard to keep up a friendship when you're sick in bed or in the hospital all of the time. Most of my friends didn't drive so it wasn't like they could just drop by and see me. Most of them didn't want to bother me. It is a nice sentiment, but it only worked to deepen my isolation from the "normal" world. If adults don't know what to say, how in the world is an adolescent going to feel comfortable finding the right words? So for the most part they stayed away, not because they didn't love me, but because they were scared. They were scared of making me feel worse, scared of facing a reality that challenged the mythology of indestructibility, and yes, some were even scared they might catch it. Seriously, at one point I heard about a rumor going around school that I wouldn't be allowed to come back even when I finished chemotherapy because other students might catch my cancer. Yes, it sounds stupid now, but they didn't know. You'd be surprised what teenagers are willing to accept as fact without any proof. I've had to learn over the years not to let it surprise me.

I was fortunate to have one group of friends that was an amazing exception to the rule. This group from my church never left my side. When I was well enough to go to church, they treated me like I was the biggest VIP to ever enter the building. They took care of me without making me feel helpless. They called me. They took pictures of events I couldn't attend. I've never forgotten their commitment. They taught me how to be a better friend, and I still thank God for them by name.

We all had to amend our mythology together. Young people do get sick, and yes, some even die. Life is not perfect, and there are no guarantees. Sounds simple enough, but keep in mind most of us don't begin to learn those truths until we leave college and have to get a real life. It's part of growing up, but we aren't usually pushed into full maturity before we've even finished puberty. Cancer forced me to grow up, and it forced me to grow up fast.

Physically I entered menopause at age 16, in the middle of puberty. My hormones didn't know which way was up. I can remember my first hot flash, even though I didn't know at the time what it was. I thought I was dying. I was sitting in class with a nice blouse and sweater vest on, appropriate attire for late winter. Suddenly this heat wave hit me so fast I could hardly breathe.

Men should never laugh at a woman about her hot flashes. If you've never experienced one, let me give you a remote idea of what it's like. Put on all your winter clothes, sweaters, heavy socks, the works. Go to a gym and have someone heat up the sauna to full blast. Then step in and try to catch your breath. I guarantee you'll set a new record for stripping off clothes. As soon as you get down to bare minimum garments, run and lock yourself in a walk-in freezer. It's not fun! It is especially scary when you don't know what's happening to you because you're only 16.

Growing up physically was the easy part. It was the emotional aspect that really challenged me. Nobody stares down death and comes out innocent. The cancer diagnosis for me carried with it a hard hitting message about my mortality. From the moment of diagnosis on, I couldn't escape the fact that life was short. I still laughed at all the same things and liked the same foods, but some things just didn't matter anymore. My friends didn't get it. Sometimes it was hard to communicate with them. We didn't share the same focus anymore. I didn't have time for typical life drama. Life was too short.

I had to come to terms with the reality that I could die. Whether from cancer or an off-course bus, death was a certainty at some point, and every moment was precious. Many adults have yet to come to this conclusion. I had to learn to balance "I could die" with my teen belief of "I won't die." I had to find the middle ground.

For me it was a choice not to be a victim. My junior year of high school I read a poem that began, "Death be not proud." That is where I have found my balance. Death may come. It *will* come. I cannot change that, but at 16 I made a quiet promise to myself. Death will come, but when he gets here, he'll find me busy living my life. No "what if," no "what might have been." There was an element of danger in that thinking. In my immaturity I sometimes used this philosophy to justify some pretty foolish choices. Cancer forced me to grow up in some ways, but in other ways it left me as a child to deal with some pretty huge complexities of life.

Living in the Memphis area I have the privilege of seeing the level of patient care at St. Jude's Research Hospital. Many of the children and teens there are very ill, even terminal. What I love to see is how the nurses and doctors know when to treat them as mature beings able to make their own decisions about treatment and when to have wheelchair races down the hall and kick the bubble making machine into high gear.

Two weeks after I finished all my chemo, I went on the youth choir mission trip. It was a challenge, and I'm sure it was more than frightening for my parents; however, they were right there with me. It was the best medicine I had ever received. I got to be normal. No meds. No doctors. No nurses. No needles. It was just me and my friends being crazy and serving God. I distinctly remember a pretty crazy water gun fight in the hallway of the Houston Holiday Inn. My sincere apologies to the management and deepest gratitude for letting kids be kids. I hadn't been one in months.

That is one of the challenges all teens with a chronic illness face. Sometimes they are forced to make grown-up type decisions and deal with painful procedures, yet inside they are really children still trying to figure out how life is supposed to work and how they fit into it. They aren't adults, but they aren't innocents anymore either.

The afternoon I was told I had cancer again, I wrote a poem:

> *I don't want to die.*
> *I want to grow up.*
> *I want to be a lawyer.*
> *I want to have kids.*
> *I don't want to die.*

Having to face my own mortality brought about a philosophy that has shaped my whole life. Some things just don't matter in the grand scheme of life. I'll be responsible and take care of business as best I can, but I will absolutely stop everything to blow bubbles from a bottle. I will walk slowly and notice flowers and bugs. I have worried less about how recently the house has been dusted and how high the laundry pile might be and focused more on savoring every moment of every relationship. And every day I thank God that He gave me the opportunity to learn this lesson so young. I didn't waste nearly as much time as most people do.

One final challenge that teens face is the aftermath of cancer. By my seventeenth birthday, I had beaten cancer. I'd also missed a year of school, was significantly weaker than I'd ever been, and had parents that jumped every time I sneezed. To put it nicely, they were overprotective, and they had every right to be. There was a constant fear of reoccurrence. It would have been easy for me to just sit back and quit on life and nobody would have blamed me. "Poor Cara. She's had it so rough."

Now, I'm the type of person who gets really fired up when you tell me I can't do something. I'll do it to prove you wrong, even if it isn't the smartest thing in the world. Missed a year of school? I returned to school the next year and graduated with my class. I was weaker, but I was more focused and was certainly more determined. I ranked twenty-seventh out of a group of over 500.

My experience with cancer as a teenager has given me a distinct advantage in working as a high school teacher today. When I have a teenager who tells me they "can't," I point to number two on my list of classroom rules. The two words not allowed are "can't" and "won't." Don't tell me you can't. You can tell me it's hard. You can tell me you don't know how. Don't tell me you can't. I don't believe it because when I was 15, I took it out of my vocabulary. The key is to not lie down and wallow in self-pity. Make a choice to try. Make a choice to move forward. So what if life is hard? When is it not? Everyone has burdens to carry, and everyone has choices to make. The minute you allow the negative circumstances in your life to overcome you, you have died, no matter what the heart monitor says. That's my constant challenge as a cancer over-comer.

Anger

Most people expect side effects from chemo. They ask questions about them. They plan for them. It's a no-brainer: poison in your body will impact your physical condition. What many people don't consider is how much chemotherapy wreaks havoc on your emotions. Along with the chemical battle in your body, there is also a chemical battle in your brain. God designed certain chemicals, chiefly serotonin, to keep our mood swings balanced and our emotions in check. Chemotherapy has a major impact on the serotonin level which means you can add your emotions to the list of things that are completely out of your control.

My first response to cancer was to be angry. In fact, I don't think anger is a strong enough word to describe how I felt sometimes. I was mad at my body for betraying me. I did the right things, took care of myself, and all the while parts of my body were planning a mutiny. I was furious that a few rebellious cells could so radically impact my life in such a negative way. What was worse, I couldn't do anything about it.

After a while, irritation flows in from many areas. I hate being told what to do. Suddenly everyone in the world seemed to be in my face, and they wouldn't back off. My students used to say they were, "All up in my Kool-Aid and didn't even know the flavor." That is certainly how it felt. I was asked question after question; the same ones over and over again. "Did you take your medicine?" "Do you feel tired?" "Are you washing your hands to protect yourself from infection?" "How many times did you use the bathroom today?" "Did you have a bowel movement?" *People, please! A little breathing room here!* Of course I knew even then it was necessary and important, but it got old quickly.

Sometimes I slipped into self-pity and would get frustrated with my friends. Being home all day got lonely. Why didn't they call more? Why didn't they drop by more often? It was hard to see past my own illness to remember that even though my friends loved me, I wasn't necessarily the center of their speed dial universe, and that was okay. My daughter was 6 when I got breast cancer. I really had to guard against taking my anger out on her. I had always dreamed of being there for everything, and now I wasn't even allowed to brush her hair for six weeks. I couldn't go on her field trips. I was too sick to play with her much. She simply couldn't understand so she just kept asking.

My out-of-whack brain would send the message that I was a failure as a parent. I had to fight that message and the anger it brought up. I would almost strike out against her as if it was her fault. I had to live with the fact that Ashley needed a Mommy, and I wasn't a bad Mommy just because I wasn't the one brushing her hair or fixing her breakfast. We got creative on things we *could* do together. We would pile coloring books on my bed and color. She "taught" me how to play her favorite card games with her own set of rules. We watched her favorite cartoons and movies together. I even made it to a few of her t-ball games.

At that time, God taught me a lesson that I've carried forward. Our family continues to be non-traditional in our schedule and family roles; partly because of life after cancer and partly because blending a youth ministry with a high school theatre teacher and an active pre-teen leads to a deliciously chaotic life. It's not for everybody, but we love it. Having cancer taught me that "Mommy" comes in many different packages, and nobody says I have to buy the same package my mother did.

Mostly when I was angry, I was angry at God. He called me His child. He said He cared for me. He said He had a plan to prosper me, not to harm me, and this was it? Cancer a second time? A third? A fourth? A fifth? What kind of stupid plan is that?

I was fortunate enough to travel to Israel many years ago. While there, we traveled the Jericho Road between Jerusalem and Jericho; it is a desolate, steep trail never meant for a bus or car. It starts in the Jericho desert, the site of Jesus' temptation.

In His time, it was a 12 hour walk through the worst terrain I've ever seen; not enough dirt to grow a weed and evil lurking behind every rock. Steep and rough, the path climbs along the edge of the Wadi Kelt; translated it means, "The Valley of the Shadow of Death." It is so deep and narrow the sun never reaches the bottom. It was a favorite haunt for the murderous thieves who preyed on the pilgrims traveling between the Holy City and the desert below. You see, to the psalmist who penned the 23rd Psalm, the shadow was a very real place with very real dangers.

You and I are pilgrims on a journey. We each must walk the valley, and to be honest, it's a nasty road. Never mind that it's steep, and the rocks are killing your feet. The big worry is never knowing when a big something is going to climb up from the shadow and waylay you. You know the ones. They make you question yourself and your ability to climb. They make you wonder about the IQ of a God who would dream up such a crazy plan for your life. "I can't do it, and I'm a horrible person because I'm tired of trying. What a stupid plan! What a cruel God!" Murmurs from the shadows.

Yes, the valley is a very real place with real dangers, but the psalmist knew another reality. We don't make the climb alone, and light awaits us at the end. Jerusalem: The place where His name dwells ... *home*. As you round the last bend, the shadows give way to the shadow-less day of the Holy City. Big deal, you say. That's half a mountain away. True, but the Light climbs with you and longs to step between you and the shadows. The shadows won't stop coming and the rocks won't miraculously smooth out, but the Light will remind you what you are climbing for.

Does the knowledge of that day make the climb easier? The truth is, sometimes yes and sometimes no. That's reality. Does the knowledge make the anger go away? The truth is, sometimes yes and sometimes no. That's reality, but so is Jerusalem and so is the Light that climbs alongside you. You can let Him have your anger; both as you express it to Him and as you give it over to Him.

Yes, I was angry, but I learned that the anger wasn't necessarily a bad thing. Instead of letting it rule me, I channeled it into my battle. Athletes call it a game face, and that's how I deal with the anger. I don't deny it's there. That would be silly. Rather, I acknowledge and use it to my advantage. When we're angry we fight harder. The American Cancer Society had a great advertisement with Lynn Redgrave once. She said, "I refuse to die of breast cancer." I know what she means. Cancer isn't going to beat me.

Depression

Will it ever stop being hard? Will I ever feel better? Is there really any hope? These are questions I asked over and over again. The problem is that there are no answers in the midst of the battle. My brain did its best to provide some logic, but it was merely theoretical. The truth was I just couldn't know, and it dragged me into despair. I felt like a failure because I couldn't always hold on to hope. I felt like a failure because I was depressed, which depressed me even more, which led to an even more heightened sense of failure. It was a dangerous avalanche of emotion, and my inability to maintain hope wasn't the only contributing factor.

It's no surprise that depression is a part of chemotherapy. Some of the depression will be caused by the changes in your body. Some of it will be circumstantial. Even if you have a strong outlook and a good sense of humor, there will be days when it's pretty hard to fight against it.

Repeatedly in the Scriptures we see people who were tired, sad, or scared. Elijah sat in a cave wanting to die. Jonah sat under a vine pouting about how God didn't follow his plan. David, Jeremiah, Naomi, Saul: Even Jesus in the Garden of Gethsemane sweated blood because the looming obstacle was too overwhelming to face alone. Not every day can be happy sunshine. That's not reality. Reality is that some days stink. It's okay to say that, and it's okay to feel that. It's not okay to get stuck there.

Facing depression isn't bad. Giving up on your life is. It's not always an easy choice when you feel overwhelmed. It's hard to say, "Okay, enough of this. I'm tired of feeling low. Let's move on." It is, however, a choice you make. You can decide to make the most of your life with where you are at this very moment. You thank God for your depression for at least you feel something. You thank God that the day stinks. It means you have good times to contrast with the present trial. You thank God that you have another day. It may not be the day you wanted, but it is a day.

When I am feeling particularly low, I draw a great big bubble bath and have a great big cry. It helps. I have to get it out. Stuffing away feelings hurts the healing process. And while family and friends will listen, I talk to someone who's been there; who knows what I'm talking about. There is a tremendous amount of support among the cancer-overcoming family. I may also watch a funny movie or read a good book. I may go to the park and swing. The idea is to do some thing positive.

I am a person who lacks self-discipline. It's true. I even have the personality inventory scores to prove it. I am horrible at keeping up with stuff and maintaining a strict routine. This character trait provided me with an additional challenge to chemo. Cancer requires a strict routine. Medicine must be administered and monitored on a precise schedule. Some people thrive on that kind of thing: schedules, time tables, lists, strict protocols. I am not one of them. All the personal habits chemo required stretched me to new limits, and I frequently fell short. I simply couldn't keep up with it all.

Truthfully, even the most organized will struggle. Chemo slows down even the sharpest mind. You can't keep it from happening. It's how I imagine it must feel to have Alzheimer's disease. I knew I should be able to keep up with it all, but I simply couldn't. The toxins attacking my brain diminished my mental capacity. Some who know me would say there wasn't much to diminish. Be that as it may, chemo brain can drag you down into despair quickly. To be suddenly incompetent at things in which you used to excel is alarming. To be honest, it's just not fair. Cancer is ravaging the body. There's nothing that I could do about that. At least I should be able to keep a clear mind.

I remember this one moment at church. It was at the end of six stressful weeks after being sick. I missed church three weeks in a row. I was battling depression; part of it was chemical, part of it was situational. So I went to church. I made myself be there, forcing myself to participate because I knew that's what I needed. Physically, after surgery, they make you get up and walk. That's what you've got to do. It hurts. It's hard. You don't want to do it, but you know you have to make yourself if you want to get well. I made myself go to church.

I didn't hear very much, and I don't remember what the sermon was about, but at the end, the pastor used a verse that I needed to hear. I had always read II Timothy 1:7 in the New International Version Bible which says, "God has not given us a spirit of fear and timidity but of power, love and self control." On this morning, however, the pastor read from the King James Version, which translated self control as "sound mind." I've always heard the first part, power and love, but I've never paid attention to the "sound mind." It helped ease my depression by showing me that God hadn't forsaken me. He wasn't going to allow chemotherapy to destroy my brain. He wasn't setting me up to fail. It was a comforting thought for me that strengthened me when I had more "down" weeks.

Isn't it funny that we seek a pill to fix everything that's wrong with us, but when a doctor recommends an anti-depressant, we refuse to fill the prescription? The doctors tell us, "Okay, here's the plan. We're going to stick you full of needles and pump gallons of poison into your body. It's going to make you horribly sick, and I guarantee you'll feel close to death, but it might kill the cancer." And we eagerly agree to treatment. Yet, when a doctor offers us a single pill that will clear our mind, settle our anxieties, help us sleep, restore our appetite, and help us regain a grasp on hope, we balk. I certainly did. I didn't need depression meds. That was for weak people. I wasn't out of control. I could handle it. Yeah, right. All it took was three weeks on the medication, and my husband was ready to buy my doctor a steak dinner.

Think about depression from a medical rather than emotional perspective. The brain produces a chemical called serotonin. This delightful little fellow regulates emotions. Yes, that's right. Emotions are driven by chemical impulses. Don't believe me? Hang out with a group of women going through pregnancy or menopause. It will make a believer out of you and fast. When the serotonin level is not balanced, neither are the emotions. Anti-depressants return serotonin to a normal level. Different ones work in different ways, but the important fact is that they work.

Think about it this way. If my body makes too much cholesterol there is not much I can do on my own to stop it. Yes, I can alter my diet to minimize additional cholesterol, but I can't kick my body out of overdrive. Does that mean I'm a failure? Of course not. It simply means I need medical assistance. The same is true with chemo and depression. At least half of it is chemical. Don't be ashamed to tell your doctor you are struggling. Don't be ashamed to take the medication. At 90, facing blindness and grieving the loss of her husband of 72 years, my grandmother asked her doctor for anti-depressants. She announced, "I may have to be depressed, but I don't have to be a victim of it."

For some people it is a short term situation. My brain has been so ravaged that anti-depressants are a permanent part of my life. Everyone around me knows I need them, and we laugh about it. They call them my "happy pills." My doctor says they are to replace some of the chemicals I need to be balanced. I tried to tell him I've never been balanced before. Why start now?

So acknowledge that depression is a part of the experience. Getting through the low days is a struggle. Talk to your doctor. Give it to God. Your job is to get up out of the tub, dry your tears, and decide not to let the depression win.

Guilt

I have a bachelor's degree in psychology, but I still don't get how guilt works. Even with a couple of years of being professionally counseled for depression, I don't have a clue on how to get past it sometimes. I'm a sucker for it. Apparently I have a big "guilt" target painted on me. It's little old me against an entire monster offensive line of guilt, and I get tackled to the ground every time.

I think I've found everything there could possibly be to feel guilty about relating to cancer. Hey, it's a gift. I know the positive messages to use to overcome these guilt messages. I have repeated them as my mantra, but just because I knew the right things to tell myself didn't necessarily change the fact that I felt guilty. I finally reached a point where I just had to learn that guilt is a part of the whole disease process. I had to approach it from a purely clinical position. Each time I heard or felt the guilt in my head and my heart, I would prescribe a truth to combat it and move on. Sometimes that truth "pill" was effective immediately. Other times it took a cumulative dose to kick in. I learned to be consistent in the dosing, just like my regular meds.

So what could there possible be to feel guilty about? You asked, so I'm going to tell you. It starts with feeling stupid, inadequate, and feeble because you can't do the things you feel you should be able to do and up until the chemo started could do. You should be able to go shopping without being exhausted to the point of tears after one store. You should be able to carry your own bags and not have to ask help just to get the gallon milk jug from the fridge to the counter. You should be able to concentrate long enough to remember a phone number you've known for years. Yes, they are all little things, but when you've always been able to do the little things and suddenly they are monumental tasks frequently left incomplete, it gets to you.

I am a fiercely independent person. I hate being thought of as lazy, so every time someone else had to do something for me, I felt guilty. I felt like it was something I should be doing for myself. It was very hard for me to accept the truth that I just wasn't capable at that moment, and that it was okay. Breast cancer surgeries have left me permanently restricted in what I can lift. I'm not supposed to lift much, and frankly, all the surgeries have taken any arm strength I might have had anyway. I sometimes feel like my students must think I'm the laziest teacher ever. We build at least one theatrical set a semester, and I'm pointing and directing like crazy while they do all the heavy lifting. I try to help because I feel guilty, and then I feel guilty because I know I'm not supposed to be lifting. Either way I can't win!

The sheer exhaustion of cancer and chemo really dragged me into the guilt loop quickly. My life has always been a strange balance of organized chaotic schedules and stillness. It comes in spurts and I love it that way. I like to be still and quiet, but it gets old pretty quick. My husband, my daughter, and I are all go, go, go type people. It's when we're happiest. The reality of chemo is that you just can't go, go, go. It's more stay, stay, stay, and just that much activity requires frequent naps.

Even as a teen I would feel that I had failed somehow because the pace of my life had slowed. I had to learn to remind myself that the change of pace was not of my choosing. Therefore, I could not be responsible for it. I shouldn't feel guilty because guilt implies responsibility and culpability, neither of which applied. I didn't run to the front of the cancer class waving my hand in the air shouting, "Pick me! Pick me!" It slunk into my life as a silent predator and has continued to stalk me despite my best efforts.

Even so, when I still feel tired today years after my last cancer battle, it's hard to accept the truth. I will always be more tired than everybody else around me. It doesn't mean I'm a failure. It doesn't mean I'm lazy. It means I've overcome cancer, more than once, and the battle scars sometimes weigh heavy. I think for me the guilt comes most when I fear that other people think less of me because I don't do more. I'm still fighting that one, but I do know it's a lie straight from the serpent's mouth. God expects that I do nothing more or less than what He created me to do. The moment I try to be anything else I will most certainly fail. What's more, God has created me to be a cancer over-comer, and that entails being a little different than the average Jane.

When I was taking treatment, I struggled with feeling guilty for not appreciating the fact that I was still alive. There were days when I felt I just couldn't take another needle. Just driving to treatment was enough to bring me to tears. I got so tired of it. I got tired of feeling ill all the time. I got tired of the whole thing. On top of that I would feel bad that I felt so bad. You know what I mean? I was depressed about things, but then I would feel guilty about being depressed. It seemed so ungrateful to be down about anything when I was still alive. It could be worse.

When I did start getting better physically, I felt guilty that I didn't feel better quicker. I knew the guilt was unfounded, so I would get angry at myself for feeling guilty. Then I would realize that guilt was a natural part of the emotional cycle so I would feel guilty for feeling angry, then angry for feeling guilty, and then … well, you get the picture. My emotions seemed out of control, and I felt guilty about that as well. I was a mess.

The fact is that cancer and chemo will send you into a tailspin of conflicting emotions that come out of nowhere. The important thing is to know that it is supposed to happen that way. Mood swings and random thoughts are par for the course. The last thing you need to do is complicate everything with unfounded guilt.

It took a year of counseling for me to come to accept a very simple truth. Here it is. It's earth shattering so you might want to be sure you are sitting down for this one. Are you ready? You have emotions. Yes, I know. Get a sip of water and take a deep breath. It's a shocker, but it's true. What's more, you are supposed to have different emotions. That was the part that was somewhat new to me. I thought I was always supposed to feel happy and in control. Boy, did cancer trash that plan. I had to learn that a full range of emotions not only happens, but it's normal and healthy. I had to learn to give myself permission to be sad or mad or even glad.

I've grown to realize I'm not a bad person if I hate feeling sick. I'm not a bad person if I'm fed up with life after cancer and its limitations. I'm not a bad person for having a great fortieth birthday and crying in the middle of it because I get to have a fortieth birthday. Those things are all normal. I need to be concerned if I don't feel all those things. Guilt is a worthless lie I pile on myself. It is a choice I make so I simply have to choose to not do it. Did I say simply? Well, it sounds simple, but so does chemo, doesn't it? We'll just give you this medicine and the cancer will most likely go away or at least shrink. No big deal. *Yeah, right.*

So what's the cure for guilt? Keep giving yourself permission to feel whatever it is you're feeling. Embrace it as a sign that life is still normal in the midst of medical chaos. Most importantly, remember it's not your fault.

Uncertainty

One of the hardest questions to answer when dealing with cancer is, "How are you?" What are you supposed to say? Does the inquirer want the short or the long answer? Does she want the medical update or the emotional forecast? I got into the bad habit of saying nothing or giving the full medical report. I never have been able to find a happy medium. I think it would probably be in the listener's best interest for me to give them a multiple choice response. "How am I has four possible responses. Please choose from the following menu: A. Medical updates, B. Physical well-being, C. Emotional response, or D. All of the above."

The thing is that people have to know that it is okay to ask. Not knowing what to ask keeps people from asking at all. That makes the patient feel isolated. Give people permission to ask. When someone says, "How are you?" give them an answer. Let them know you want to talk, but ask them how much they want to hear.

I'll never forget having to tell my daughter that I had breast cancer. She was 6, and I took her to her favorite restaurant, just the two of us. As we ate I tried to tell her that I was sick, and I would be taking medicine that would make me even sicker for a while. I prayed so hard every moment, and God gave me some good advice. "Answer her questions. If she asks, tell her. If she needs to know, tell. She is just as uncertain as you are and just as afraid of the unknown as you are."

Sometimes I think cancer is harder for those around the patient than it is for the patient. I often lost sight of that when I was in the midst of things. Trying to help my daughter through my breast cancer really brought it home. I was always unsure of how much she needed to know. I didn't want to overwhelm her, but I wanted her to be prepared; the less surprises the better. It was a special time for us. I learned how to communicate with my child, and we learned together how to talk about things. In many ways it was a beautiful time because she learned she can ask me anything, and I will try my best to answer her. She felt secure because I trusted her with information. Of course, I didn't burden her with anything really heavy, but when my hair fell out, she knew it was coming and why.

One of the hardest parts of cancer, it seems to me, is the not knowing. The uncertainty applies to every aspect. "I don't know what I have. I don't know how to treat it. I don't know if the treatment will work. I don't know that it won't come back again." There is a major unknown at every turn.

As I write this page I am celebrating my fortieth birthday. I've frequently joked that I did cancer twice in my teens, twice in my twenties, once in my thirties, and the forties is going to be my cancer-free decade. I've been weaning myself off it, and now I'm ready to quit cold turkey. It sounds funny, but as I write I find that my eyes are leaking. I'm not sad. It honestly is just another day in my life. The thing is, how many times was there not supposed to be another "day in my life?" I shouldn't have lived to be 20, 30 seemed a miracle, and here I sit at 40. Is it too much to hope that the cancer is really gone for good? I'd like to think so, but the reality is I don't have any say in the matter. I've certainly let God know my personal position on the topic. Yet, I look at the decade in front of me knowing that every visit to the doctor has the potential to put my life into another tailspin or be another cause for celebration.

The uncertainty can eat you alive. I've made a choice. That seems to be a theme in my life, but nevertheless, that is the best word for it. I choose. I choose to acknowledge that the fear of cancer returning is real. I choose to acknowledge that I have no control over how my body may or may not choose to mutate on me next. I choose to continue to do all the things my doctors tell me to do to live as healthy a life as possible in a world where my favorite foods will always be pizza and fries. I choose to live today for today and leave tomorrow for tomorrow. I choose to be 40 and 41 and 42 and maybe even 43. So the rest of the world can choose to sit back or to run with me, but don't lie down in my lane because I will run you over. It's the one thing I know for certain.

Chemotherapy's
Spiritual Effects

Living in God's Lap

When you're 13 you don't think about being sick, much less dying. Maybe that's why that first time I never fully understood the big "C" word, even through all the surgeries and treatments. I don't know what I thought I had. All I can remember knowing is that I had a tumor, and it needed to be removed. Then I needed radiation to make sure it didn't grow back. It seemed like no big deal to me. God must have really protected my brain from it. I can remember my parents being upset, but somehow it never sunk in.

The tumor was located on my thymus gland directly beneath my sternum. It was the size of a grapefruit with tendrils growing toward the lymph glands in my neck. In order to remove it, it was necessary to crack my sternum apart, similar to open heart surgery. When I came out of surgery I lived in the thoracic ICU for three days. I was the only person in there under the age of 55. My mother had pulled some strings and managed to stay by my side 24 hours a day.

I only have one clear memory of those days. My father was a music minister at First Baptist Church in Garland, Texas. His youth choir had been planning a trip, and they were scheduled to leave for Georgia three days after my surgery. Sometime during my ICU stay my father came to my bedside. He held my hand and asked for my permission to leave on his trip. He said, "If you want me to stay, I'll stay. Someone else can take my place."

Of course I told him to go, but I think that is when I began to realize for the first time that this thing going on in my body might be a bigger deal than they were all letting on. The thing that struck me most was Daddy *asking* me if he could go. I mean, he's the head of the family. He's the one who makes the decisions. Of course, I understand now that it was his way of telling me and Mom that he loved us and would never leave us to deal with life on our own.

I've been blessed with parents who have taught me about God just by the way they live their lives. That day I began learning a very important lesson about my Heavenly Father. He'll do whatever it takes to stay by my side, no matter what it costs Him. There were no day beds in ICU so I'm not exactly sure where my mother slept, or if she really slept at all. I just know that every time I opened my eyes, she was immediately visible. Even if I just spoke her name, she was instantly there.

God's that way. We don't think about it. We just kind of take it for granted. I mean, of course, He's there. He's God. But think about it. He's *there*. I mean, *here,* and it cost Him everything. He gave up His glory, His throne, His very life so that every moment of every day He could be here beside me through every insignificant event, every crisis, and every celebration. All I need do is open my heart's eyes, and He becomes immediately visible; speak His name, and He instantly responds, "Yes, my beloved child?" And He never goes away, ever.

There have been some pretty tough times in my life that my father has not been there for. Let's face it, I'm not Daddy's little girl anymore. He doesn't build his life around me. Yet, God is my Abba, my Daddy. He tells me in Psalm 134 that He is obsessed with me, consumed with thoughts of me. His love letter to me tells me that He built His entire eternity around me, making sure that we could be together forever. More than once I have run to Him and crawled up in His lap. The fabulous thing about God being your Daddy is that you never get too big to sit in His lap, and your problems are never too big for Him to fix.

Now that I look at it, maybe that's why I wasn't concerned about the surgeries and treatments. My parents had taught me, even at the age of 13, to live in the lap of God. Of course, I didn't stay there. We never do, do we? Once life calms down, we think it's safe to jump down and run off on our own again. I wonder if God ever gets tired of me running off, scraping my knees, and running back to Him.

My family and the doctors were always careful not to use the word "cancer." I could tell you all about Hodgkin's disease, lymphoma, and various medical tests. I was quite the medical dictionary as a seventh grader. It wasn't until later that I slowly became aware that I had been treated for cancer. There wasn't a huge "Aha!" moment. It just gradually dawned on me. But when it finally crystallized in my mind, the fear set in. I had cancer! Cancer kills people. In the late 1970's, getting cancer of any kind was an automatic death sentence, or so it seemed. I had escaped death. You'd think I would be spending my time rejoicing over that, but no. I'm not that smart. Or maybe I'm just human?

I spent the next three years living in fear that the cancer would come back. My mind was constantly plagued by what ifs. What if it comes back? What if they can't treat it? What if it kills me? Every doctor's visit was terrifying. I never told anybody how afraid I was. I think I believed that if I said it out loud, it was certain to happen; however, if I kept it to myself I might just get by it. It's kind of like pulling the covers over your head to fool the monsters into searching some other bedroom for a juicy child to devour. Sure enough, my worst nightmare came true. It came back. I'd been worrying for three years, waiting for the other shoe to drop, and it finally did … hard!

There's a certain peace in hitting rock bottom. At least you know it can't get any worse. It's certainly easier to find God there. I was forced to make the decision of whether or not I would trust God. Faith isn't a feeling so trusting God can't be based on mood swings. Faith is a fact. Regardless of the situation, God's power, character, and providence won't change. I decided God was bigger than me, and He knew the plan so I would just let Him take care of things. I can't tell you how I made that decision. It just came naturally to me. I truly believe it was the Holy Spirit. It was just a no-brainer. I wasn't in charge; God was. I didn't have control; God did. I didn't have to understand. I just had to trust.

I'm not really quick at picking up on subtle lessons so God always seems to opt to make things really plain for me. If cancer hadn't come back, some other major test or trial would have. Just because He loves me, just because I try to live in His lap, doesn't mean that I get special favors. Life is going to happen, and sometimes it comes at you pretty fast. That's life. It's not about what happens; it's about what you do with what happens. It's about who you turn to and where you choose to focus. And you will make a choice so you might as well think about it.

I've come to the conclusion that nobody is going to come out of this life alive. Think about it. Fortunately, my Jesus has conquered death and the grave. Why in the world would I want to spend my time worrying about dying? I've got some living to do. In fact, I think getting cancer for a second time was perhaps the best thing that ever happened to me. Who knows how long I would have been afraid to live because I might die. There's a faulty piece of logic for you.

So, I choose to live my life. Rather, I live in the lap of God, and we live my life together. Sometimes I think God's lap is like sitting in a rocking chair, and other times I'm pretty sure we're going over Niagara Falls in a barrel. Life's an adventure. Don't be afraid to live it.

Preparing for Your Battle

You've been diagnosed, and you're trying to wrap your mind around what is happening to you. It's a legitimate question to ask God about what's going on. But you need to understand; you may not get an answer. This may not be what you want to hear. We live in a society that says it's all about me. It's what I like, what I want to do, and when I want to do it. But God says it's not about us, and He doesn't have to answer us one bit. That's a hard reality. It's harsh. We're called to a faith, and faith means I don't necessarily get the "whys."

So you say, "Okay, I've been diagnosed with cancer. I want to know why." God says, "I want you to trust Me." "No, God. That's not the deal. That's not the arrangement we had." And God says, "Oh, yes. That's My covenant. I don't know what covenant you signed but the covenant of My blood says My blood's good enough and you don't need answers." It's hard to live like that.

That's why chapter 55 of the Book of Isaiah has always been so significant to me. God says, "Look, you're not ever going to understand." It ends in a promise. God says, "My ways are higher than your ways. My thoughts are not your thoughts. My Word is not going to return to Me empty. It's going to do exactly what I want, to achieve the purpose for which I've sent it, and *you will go out in joy.* Look, you're not going to understand it, but you can accept the fact that whether you feel like it or not, I know what I'm doing, and I'm going to take care of you. I have plans to prosper you and not to harm you." Can't you just hear God saying that?

This is where I learned I've got to know my scripture. I simply would not have made it through cancer without my Bible. I don't care how many counselors I had, how strong my family support was, or if I even had Billy Graham for a pastor. Scripture was my weapon. My weapon against the disease was the medicine they gave me. My weapon against the emotional issues was knowledge about the disease, but my real weapon was scripture.

It goes back to Ephesians 6, your spiritual armor. Here's your sword. *All right, I've got to do battle because Satan is trying to destroy me spiritually right now.* It would be really easy to give in because you're fighting a legion, and you're standing there alone. Until, that is, you pick up the Bible and you realize, "Okay, Job might not have had cancer, but he fought the same battle. Elijah didn't have cancer, but he fought the same battles spiritually and emotionally."

Chapters 11 and 12 of Hebrews show that we are surrounded by a great cloud of witnesses … people who have had cancer, who have had all these things that we've had, who have gone before us, and they're saying, "You can do it! Here, look at this passage." The Bible isn't about giving us the whys. Sometimes you'll get a why, but you're not going to get a lot. Scripture for me is not about finding out the whys. It's about finding the facts about God and His consistency time after time after time from the beginning of time, and then comparing that to His consistency in my life time after time after time. In my life it's to know this reality: He's not going to fail me.

In the spiritual sense, you will either come out of crisis closer to God or farther away, but you can't come out at the same spot you went in. It just doesn't happen. You will always look at God differently. Be honest with yourself about your thoughts and feelings. Be honest with God. He can handle it. He can be trusted because He loves you. Allow yourself to work through the questions, and you'll find that your life in and after cancer can be joyful and satisfying.

What you believe about God will color your experiences both during cancer treatment and in the days that follow as you determine your new "normal" life. If you believe God has failed you, is punishing you, or isn't all-powerful after all, you will find yourself going it on your own. You will, of course, come out farther from God. If you believe that God is with you in the midst of everything and will keep His promises, you can experience a closeness with Him you never knew was possible. It's your choice, but it's much easier facing the future with God than without Him. Trust me on this.

I'll Be Home for Christmas (1983)

Holidays are hard when you're sick. You feel like you just have to sit and watch it all pass you by. You can't even enjoy the food because chemo has done one or more of four things: taken away your appetite, given you mouth sores, changed the way everything tastes, or made it impossible to keep anything down.

My family, as most families, had very specific traditions for Christmas, and they all revolved around traveling to my grandparents' farm in New Mexico. We never missed a holiday on the farm. However, that tradition was in danger the Christmas of 1983. The big question was whether or not my white counts would be solid enough for me to make the trip. So I started praying for my Christmas miracle. I was so sick that I was sure God owed me at least this one thing. *At least give me Christmas. I'm going through all this for You and with You, God. You at least owe me Christmas.*

I have this mental picture of God. All I can see is His mouth and it's permanently fixed in this bemused, patient grin. I say many stupid things, most of them to God. I'm certain I'm an unending source of amusement to Him, and Christmas of my sixteenth year was no exception. I think you can probably see where this is going. Christmas approached, and my counts held. My miracle! God answered my prayers. Of course, I didn't know I was supposed to be praying for no ice storms either.

Airports closed, our annual pilgrimage was cancelled at the last minute, and I was mad. I was beyond mad; I was furious. How dare God do this to me? Now there would be no Christmas, and yes, I said it. *It just isn't fair!*

It happens that way sometimes. I tell God I trust Him with the plan. Then I hand Him my plan, and He just smiles that little smile He has for me. Well, God didn't follow my plan so I began to pout. I became, by choice, the very definition of a teenage drama queen.

"I'll Be Home for Christmas" was my theme song, and I played it over and over to remind my family I wouldn't be. I cried. I moped. I made a royal pain of myself. I had prayed that God would carry me through Christmas, and now there wouldn't be one. But you know Christmas still came. In spite of the Grinch I had become, it came just the same.

On Christmas Eve, my parents and brother attended the candlelight service at our church. I was left at home. Cold weather is a major health risk to those on treatment. Daddy built up the fire, Mom tucked me into the recliner with snacks and blankets, and off they went. I prepared for the biggest pity party in history. We do that, don't we? We gear up for it. But just as we take a deep breath for that first big wail, God says, "Hold on a second." If we're wise, we pull up short and listen. By the light of the fire and Christmas tree lights, God began to tell me a few things. It was a long conversation.

Christmas isn't about tradition. It's not even about family, at least not an earthly family. Christmas is about God's family: Jesus. It is not about me. Well, it is only in so far as God wants me to be part of His family. Christmas is about God answering my prayer for hope and life. I heard God tell me that night that He had answered my prayer for a Christmas 2000 years earlier because He knew I would need a promise of new life and future in 1983. What an amazing God! I felt small and foolish … and profoundly, deeply loved.

I hadn't been able to shop so I had no gifts for my parents. It was another thing I had pouted about. So, I sat and wrote a letter to them; the only gift I could give—an expression of my love, the gift God had given me. I told them what I had learned that night about family and asked their forgiveness for not realizing how difficult the changes must have been for them.

Exchanging gifts that night was a quiet affair, done only by firelight. Cancer drains the pocketbook as much as it does the body. Packages were scarce, but I can't remember a sweeter fellowship. It was the first year I really celebrated Christmas. I'm happy to say it wasn't the last, but the beautiful thing is that God answers the small prayers, too.

Christmas day was spent with our friends in their home. It was great fun with lots of laughter. Toward evening, I grew tired. By the time we got home that night, my fever had climbed to 104 degrees. Fever means infection and that means immediate hospitalization. So after a game of phone tag with my doctor, we packed my bag and headed toward Baylor Hospital over very icy, deserted highways. I felt really weak and didn't complain. I was just disappointed because I really wanted to make it through Christmas. When the ER doctor confirmed I would have to be admitted, I turned to Mom and asked the time. It was 12:56am on December 26, 1983. God had brought me through Christmas.

Yes, He answered my plan in His own way. And then, typical of the "more than I can ask or imagine" God I know and love, He blasted the sides out of the small box I had put Him in. "That's it?" He asks. "That's all you want? Okay, but I have so much more for you." Kablam! What's it going to take for you to let God out of His box, to see beyond your boundaries, color outside the lines?

God will take you there, but the only way is through the fire or walking on a stormy sea. I look down sometimes and start to sink, like that Christmas, or I want to hold a sit down strike in the midst of the flames. So Jesus stands there patiently waiting for my eyebrows to singe. And when I hop up with the seat of my pants smoking, He gently takes me by the hand, walks me through the hottest part I can stand, and sits me down safely in the cool of the other side. And He loves me so much He even makes my eyebrows grow back.

Many Christmases have come and gone: each unique it its own way. I've never forgotten that Eve sitting by the fire, just God and me. The degree of tenderness I felt from Him has remained crystal clear in memory regardless of how much chemo is clouding my brain. It is only with the wisdom of hindsight that I realize 1983 might have been the only year I've ever *truly* been home for Christmas.

Pattern of the Psalms

People always ask me how I do it. "How do you keep laughing? How do you keep such a positive attitude? You are so upbeat. Don't you ever get down?" The answer to the latter is a resounding, *"Yes!"* I get down often.

Depression is a natural response to life. I used to feel guilty that I wasn't "happy" all the time. If Jesus is in me, His joy should always show, right? I tried so hard to manufacture it. I've given off so much fake joy, it's ridiculous. "I'm fine." That's what I thought was the number one and only appropriate answer to "How are you?" I would smile and lie. I would even lie to God, but He knew the truth and was determined to bring me to a point of honesty in my relationship with Him.

It was October of 2001, and just when I thought things in my life couldn't get any worse, God got creative. He's good at that, you know. We were deeply in debt from a house that wouldn't sell. The tiny town we lived in had no jobs that paid above minimum wage. My husband had been falsely accused of embezzling from our church. My daughter had been sent home from school because another child's head lice had jumped ship into my daughter's clean hair. To top it off, my doctors thought they had found a new tumor. We all go through periods like that, times when it seems everything around us is wrong. Nope, life couldn't get any worse.

In the midst of this turbulent period, God softly whispered Habakkuk 1:5. "Look ... and watch ... I'm going to do something ... you would not believe even if you were told." And lightning struck our refrigerator. That's right. It was one of those crazy Oklahoma thunderstorms that rolled through and our fridge caught fire. No one was home, and it burned itself out inside the freezer; however, I came home to a house that smelled like smoke. I walked into the kitchen to find my husband throwing away all our food. There wasn't money to replace it.

What would you do? I marched straight into my backyard and proceeded to yell at God. I told Him how much I hated His plan, how stupid I thought it was, and how abandoned I felt. Didn't He love me anymore? Didn't He care? Did He even know how bad things were? We had no food!

I walked around the yard shouting my frustrations to the heavens. I'm sure the neighbors thought I'd lost my mind. After a half hour of ranting and raving and tears, something amazing happened. God didn't strike me dead. In fact, He lifted my eyes to the sky. Above the church directly behind our house was a complete double rainbow. I felt lower than a worm. It was as if God was saying, "Yes, I know. Yes, I'm here. Yes, I love you, and my child, for every hardship I have a double blessing."

"All right," I mumbled, "but it had better be a good one." God smiled, patted me on the head, and sent me inside. Three days later, a new refrigerator and freezer full of food arrived. Oh, my daughter's head lice went away, too.

When I was diagnosed with cancer this last time, my best friend and I had just started reading through the Psalms. It's a beautiful book, but I didn't quite get it. I could never figure out why David would write all these songs that sounded so much like country western music. You know … my girl left, the dog died, and my truck broke down in the rain. Of course, David's are more … my sons hate me, my country is in ruin, I'm living in a cave, and people want to kill me. Yeah, really catchy tune for church, don't you think? Then, at the end of every one of those real downers, David comes back around to, "But I love You, God, and I'm going to worship You." How did he do that? It always seemed so random to me. But I think I finally get it.

God knows we can't ignore all the bad things in our life. He never expects us to. He did, however, give us a huge book in the Bible to teach us how to deal with it. Go ahead and cry out. It's natural. Yeah, life stinks. It's hard. The odds are against me. I'm tired. The trick is not only to cry "out." We must cry "up." That's where David had one up on the country western singers. He knew to lift up his eyes to the hills. He knew the strong right hand of the Lord would protect him. He knew who would vanquish all his foes and restore him with blessings.

God doesn't mind when we go to Him. I'm pretty sure He loves it, or He wouldn't encourage us to read the Psalms. We can be honest with Him; as honest as David was. It's scary. He could strike you with lightening if you tell Him you think the plan is stupid, but He won't. I promise. I should know. I've told Him plenty of times. You know what He does? He changes our focus. Now, He can't do that until you admit to Him what your focus is. Crying out to God is saying, "All I see right now is me, and everything about me stinks!" Only then can God place a gentle finger under our chin and raise our eyes to Him. Only then, when we've been honest with ourselves and Him, can He change our focus. And man, what a difference! For a brief moment there's that glimpse of heaven, and my life is suddenly no big deal. I see God and all His glory for just a split-second, and I completely forget about myself. That's worship! That's what David learned. That's what we can learn, too.

Passing It On

◆

Jerry's Story

Stark white walls. Light grey tile with dark speckles. Pale plastic blinds. Flowers and cards are nice, but they don't do much to brighten up a hospital room. Still there I was again, 16 and sick from the latest round of chemotherapy. The cancer I had faced at 13 was back with a vengeance. While my friends were hanging out at the mall and talking about prom dates, I was losing my hair and my lunch. The doctors were bringing me to the brink of death in the hope it would save my life. All I knew was I was tired, I felt lousy, and I wanted to go home.

Into the midst of this strolled my youth pastor, Jerry Solomon. The first thing a person noticed about Jerry was the huge glasses that seemed to hide his face. They were hopelessly out of style and the butt of many youth jokes, but they also magnified the kindness and mischief in his eyes. He was a mixture of energetic intensity with soft-spoken gentleness. He was quick to laugh and quick to love. He had often visited me in the hospital. On this day, though, he brought me something that I was too sick to appreciate. Later I would realize that this extraordinary man had given me something that would change my life, a new perspective.

He marched over to my bed. "I've been asking God why this is happening to you," he announced.

Me, too! I thought.

"I can't give you an answer about why this happened, but God did show me what He intends to do with it." He opened his Bible and showed me 2 Corinthians 1:3-4. "God ... comforts us in all our troubles, so that we can comfort those ... with the comfort we ourselves have received from God." It was the first time I had seen those verses.

"I don't know how God's going to use this in your life, but it's going to be huge."

A tiny seed of hope was planted. *You mean God can use this scary, lonely, painful time in my life to bring about something good?* It's true that God had brought me comfort in many ways. There was my mom who never left my side. My dad was strong and supportive. My church, my friends, and even the doctors and nurses did their best to comfort me. Maybe God really did have a purpose for the cancer. But how would I be able to comfort others? I certainly wanted to stick around to find out.

Within a year I was back in school and getting on with my life. Jerry found ways to get me involved in the youth group. He gave me leadership positions to help me grow. He showed me how to study the Bible in-depth and how to live what I learned. He believed in me and supported me. It was Jerry I turned to for wisdom and guidance when I began working with the youth in my church during college. And when the unthinkable happened, and I had to battle cancer two more times in my twenties, Jerry was there to encourage and remind me that God had a purpose in all of it. *Comfort others with the comfort you have received.*

I had been in ministry about a year when one of my students tried to commit suicide. I went to see Jerry who spent several days teaching me from the Word and from life. "You can't fix kids," he said. "All you can do is be there to help pick up the pieces, to support, and love them. But you can't fix them." Loving my "kids" became my ministry goal. *Comfort them with the comfort you had received.*

Several years went by. I moved several times, married, adopted my daughter, and continued working with teenagers. Then one summer day I was talking with some kids at youth camp when my phone rang. It was my mother.

"I thought you would want to know that Jerry has pancreatic cancer. It doesn't look good."

I sunk to the ground feeling like I had just been given a blow in a boxing ring. *Jerry has cancer? That can't be right. He's so healthy. He was laughing and joking the last time I saw him.* What do I do? Do I go see him as quickly as possible? Part of me wanted to run to him and comfort him. Another part of me wanted to run away. It didn't seem he would receive healing this side of heaven. How would I be able to say good-bye?

It was several months before I could bring myself to make the trip to see Jerry. I stood outside his door. *Lord, I need strength. I feel so guilty. I'm healthy, and he's dying. Lord, why him? Why not me?* With a deep breath, I pushed the door open and walked into his living room. He looked the same; a little thinner maybe, but he still had those huge glasses. We talked about my mission trip to Africa, the church camp, and the kids we were reaching. We talked of everything except the most obvious. Finally he looked intently at me. His voice was weary and soft. "How do you do this?"

What could I say? I desperately wanted to have an answer for him, the man who had always had an answer for me. I knew how to live with cancer, but I didn't know how to die. *Comfort him with the comfort you have received.* I shared with him things that I had learned to get through each day: make of list of the good things that happen; find things to laugh at; surround yourself with supportive people; think of things you can do for others. Then I reminded him of what he had always told me: God has a purpose for this, too.

He slowly nodded his head in understanding and gave me a tired smile. And over the next few weeks as he grew weaker in his body, he grew stronger in his spirit. When people came to see him, he sensed they had come to say good-bye. He had one last chance to tell them something, and that something was always Jesus. This amazing man who showed me why I had cancer showed me how to die with it.

A few weeks before Christmas, Jerry was gone. On the way to the funeral, my dad handed me his Bible. "I'm going to have a devotional time with the choir. Would you read these verses?"

I opened the Bible to the passage that was marked: *2 Corinthians 1:3-4.*

The lump in my throat made it hard to swallow, and tears blurred my vision. I had come full circle in my relationship with Jerry. It was a few minutes before I could speak and tell my dad about how the first time I had read those verses was when Jerry shared them that day in the hospital so long ago. They had become my purpose. I lived them every day.

It's been several years since Jerry left us. I started teaching at the high school. One of my students was dying from a brain tumor. *Comfort him with the comfort you have received.* A friend's mother was diagnosed with cancer, and she didn't know what to do. *Comfort her with the comfort you have received.* When I went through a fifth cancer, I shared my experiences with an e-mail family made up mostly of people I'd never met but that could relate to my stories. *Comfort them with the comfort you have received.*

I still miss Jerry. I miss talking with him, getting his advice on what a Bible passage means, or how to handle a situation with one of my youth. But I have never forgotten the greatest lesson he taught me: God never wastes an experience. He has a purpose for each one, and He'll use them if we will let Him. Just as we live for Him, we can die in Him. And when we come through the trials, we can comfort those with the comfort we have received. *Thanks, Jerry.*

Breast Cancer:
A Little Different than
the Rest

Mammograms

My brother has a doctorate in philosophy. He gets deep into researching his topic, in multiple languages even. Me, I just know what they tell me on the internet. The facts are pretty clear on breast cancer. Statistics now show that one in four women will contract breast cancer during her lifetime. That's a pretty scary statistic. Think about it this way. If a woman has two daughters, it is highly probable that if she doesn't get breast cancer someone in her immediate family will. I was diagnosed with infiltrating ductile carcinoma. That's fancy talk for, "If we don't cut off your chest and make you sick for the next several months, you will die."

Breast cancer is a little different than other cancers. I suppose it can be likened to prostrate cancer for men in that people are much more uncomfortable asking about it. The instant I told someone I had breast cancer one of two things happened; they either looked down at my chest, or they looked away trying not to look at my chest. I know what they were thinking. "Are those her real ones? Has she had surgery yet? Are those fake ones that she can take out or ones she's had redone by surgery?" I actually found it quite funny. I saw a t-shirt once that had an arrow pointing up and the text beneath it read, "My eyes are up here." That's how I felt sometimes.

My cancer was initially detected in the typical way. I felt a small lump in my right breast, so I decided it was time to have a mammogram. I had never had one before. I was successfully living in a certain state of denial that claimed if I never had a mammogram, then I would never have breast cancer. It made sense to me. Still, with my history I knew I couldn't bury my head in the sand on this one.

If you've never had the pleasure of a mammogram and you are a woman, you are in for a treat. You need to have it, and you need to go in with a big sense of humor. If you're a man, just imagine taking a pair of your most treasured anatomy pieces and putting them through these paces. A mammogram is a simple concept. Take a picture of the tissue. Of course, breast tissue isn't clear, but the wonderful world of science has an answer for that. Squish them! I honestly did not know it was possible to pinch and flatten a part of my body that much. I was truly amazed. French chefs train for years to make crepes that thin! I kept waiting for someone with a spatula to come out and flip me. I couldn't help but laugh.

Once it was over I was asked to wait in a little room, still clothed in that lovely paper blouse that is all the rage at diagnostic imaging salons these days. As I sat in my cubicle, I kept telling myself that I didn't have breast cancer. When they came and got me to do an ultrasound because they had a "question" about something, I kept telling myself that I didn't have breast cancer. When they took me back in for another mammogram to get "better" images, I kept telling myself that I didn't have breast cancer. Keep in mind my existing medical history, not to mention my knowledge of the statistics. Math was not on my side in this one, but I refused to give in. They gave me back my clothes and sent me on my way.

All the way down the interstate I kept telling myself that I didn't have breast cancer. When they called me and told me I needed to schedule a biopsy of a questionable mass, I kept telling myself that I didn't have breast cancer. It could be anything, right? I had myself so deep in denial by the time of the procedure I actually fell asleep during the biopsy. Mind you, this is a local anesthetic procedure. No sedation necessary. Most women are extremely anxious about the biopsy. Not me. The nurse told me I actually snored, probably because I wasn't sleeping at home because I was working so hard to keep telling myself that I didn't have breast cancer. I kept telling myself all the way up to the moment the biopsy doctor called. "You have breast cancer." I blame it on the mammogram. I'm sure I didn't have it until they smashed me around. It's entirely the machine's fault.

It's funny how you can try so hard to believe something and all the while know it's not true. It's like when I started to suspect that Santa Claus and my Grandmother were more closely connected than I had originally believed. I knew, but I refused to know. This was the same. I knew I had breast cancer, but I refused to know. I think that is what made waiting for that call so hard. Just once I wanted my heart to win out over my head. I'd lost out on the tooth fairy, the Easter bunny and Santa. Couldn't I just have this one?

In the end, though, I believe bad news is better than no news. At least now I knew what I was dealing with. It wasn't a happy fact, but facts are much easier to work with than myths and legends, and the fact of the matter is, I had breast cancer before I had my mammogram. Strange enough it was a lump in my right breast that took me to the doctor in the first place, but that lump turned out to be nothing. It was a much smaller mass in my left breast that turned out to be cancer. It wasn't even large enough to detect by touch yet. I've decided that maybe the human crepe making machine isn't such a bad gizmo after all.

Mastectomies

◆

The Physical Aspect

Cancer changes you. It leaves you different in many ways. However, very few cancers lead to a physical alteration to the extent that breast cancer does. From the time girls hit pre-pubescence, we are waiting for our chests to grow. Breast enhancement is a billion dollar industry. Everything in the American and European culture tells us that our womanhood is defined by childbearing and our cup size. Now, because of a double mastectomy, I suddenly found myself un-defined.

As soon as I was diagnosed with my biopsy I found the best oncologist in the region. I set up an appointment and arrived at the arranged time with my entourage in tow. There I sat in the exam room with my parents, my husband, and my typed medical history. I was ready. This doctor was going to find out very quickly that I wasn't your average cancer patient. What I look for in a doctor is someone who is aggressive in treating the disease. I'm naturally assertive, which is my husband's polite way of saying I'm bossy. I'm also a fighter, and I expect my doctor to be the same way.

When Dr. Kurt Tauer walked in the room he immediately did something that impressed me. He took out a tape recorder and taped our entire meeting. Of course, I had come prepared to take notes, but he didn't know that. He started out making sure all my questions were answered. I knew from the start this was my guy. I handed him my rather extensive medical history that I had typed up. I then proceeded to tell him what I wanted.

Even though the cancer had only been found in a small amount in one breast, I wanted a double mastectomy and while we were at it, I wanted a full hysterectomy. You may think that sounds a little drastic, but I saw it this way. If one part of my breast was already cancerous, the party was only going to get bigger, and if estrogen was involved in any way, my useless womb was nothing more than a ticking time bomb waiting to explode. I wanted to be proactive. I'm tired of chasing after cancer. This time I wanted to cut it off at the pass. *I've done Hodgkin's*

71

disease twice and I've done thyroid cancer twice. I intend to do breast cancer only once. He agreed, and just like that, it was settled. The decision seemed easy, so how hard could the actual procedure be?

Don't let my tone fool you. Mastectomies come at a price, physically and emotionally. The easy part is the physical, and keep in mind "easy" is a relative term here. If you are facing this type of surgery, I don't want to scare you. I feel the need to be honest about what I went through, but let me preface it with this truth: I went *through* it. I am not there any longer, and every breast cancer survivor I have met has also gone *through* it. You will get past this time in your life, so please don't be overcome by anything you read or hear. Don't give cancer that victory in your life.

The moment I came out of anesthesia I felt like I had been beaten with a baseball bat. I won't lie. I hurt. I hurt a lot, but Demerol® and Morphine® are wonderful things, and soon the pain was under control. There are some tips to making yourself more comfortable. A friend of mine, also a breast cancer survivor, brought me two baby pillows. She told me that if I would keep them under my elbows to keep my arms slightly propped it would alleviate some of the pressure on my chest and ease the pain. She was right.

When you have a mastectomy you can't raise your arm above your head for several weeks. For the first two weeks, I could hardly raise it to my nose. This meant arrangements had to be made for my hair. Before surgery I braided it as tightly as I could, and that lasted about five days. After that, my mother washed and brushed it for me until I could do it myself by leaning over the sink. If you are making plans for this type of surgery, I would recommend investing in pajamas that button rather than pull over. I went for satin ones so it would be easier to slide in and out of bed. The little things can really make a difference.

One thing your doctor may or may not tell you much about is a condition called lymphodemia. Looking it up online will give you a much better definition that I can, but I'll give a brief overview. As I understand it, the lymph system produces white blood cells which fight disease. The production centers are located in the lymph nodes in your neck, arm pits, and groin. When you are sick, the nodes kick into overdrive, and this is why your neck may be swollen and sore when you have a bad cold.

Many types of cancer spread throughout the body through the lymph system. This is particularly true of breast cancer, so when a mastectomy is performed, the doctor will often take a few lymph nodes from the appropriate arm pit for a biopsy. If they show up clear it is good news. The cancer has not spread. If the nodes show positive for cancer, then a doctor can better plan what type and how aggressive follow-up treatment needs to be. Doctors are really good to explain this part, but there are things that aren't always made clear.

The nodes in the armpit move fluid through your arm. Fewer nodes mean a diminished capacity to move that fluid and to fight infection in that arm. This means the arm needs to be protected; otherwise, it can swell, and that swelling will not go away. Many women have to wear special wraps and sleeves because proper precautions were not taken.

Some of the main rules are: don't lift anything heavier than five pounds with that arm, ever; I mean ever. Don't garden without a glove on that hand. Don't carry your purse on that arm. Don't allow anyone to take blood pressure on that arm. Don't ever, under any circumstance, allow a needle stick on that arm. There are many medical explanations for what causes it, but not being a doctor, I hesitate to try to explain it for fear of getting it wrong. The bottom line is: ask about it, prepare for it, and follow the rules. If you do, you will have no problems at all. It is not life threatening, at least I don't understand it to be, but it is life-style altering; you need to plan for it. If you don't, you will have major complications that could have been avoided. Do I always follow the rules? I didn't used to.

What finally got my attention was the day I sanded a piece of furniture so I could refinish it. By the time I was done my left hand was swollen so large that my ring finger was turning black. My wedding ring had cut off the circulation, and my father-in-law had to cut it off. That hand has never completely returned to its original size.

Lymphodemia is something you must take seriously if you are a breast cancer patient. When I went in for reconstructive surgery, I made a point to be sure the doctors and nurses knew not to use my left arm for anything. I had my friends, family and students take permanent markers and sign my arm all the way to the shoulder like it was a cast. Among the well wishes I wrote in large letters, "LYM-PHODEMIA—DO NOT USE THIS ARM!" I knew I could be totally out of it and not worry, and it certainly got a laugh from the operating room staff. The marker washed off as soon as I could take a good bath, and in the meantime, my arm made them and me smile.

Yes, mastectomies bring about many changes. For awhile, there are serious limitations on your life. I haven't even mentioned that I wasn't allowed to drive for six weeks. I've stated before, preparation is the key. Think ahead, and you can greatly minimize the frustrations.

Mastectomies

◆

The Emotional Aspect

If the physical aspect of a mastectomy is the "easy" part, then there is not an adjective to adequately describe the difficulty of the emotional part. I want to say again, you come *through* it. Yes, it's hard, but I'm a better person for it. Like my Granddaddy used to say, "It builds character." I thought I was a character already, but apparently God saw it differently.

It's interesting how two lumps of tissue can so completely define how you see yourself and how you believe others see you. I mean, it's just tissue, but coming to grips with letting it go was by far the most difficult thing I've ever done in my life. My hospital was a good distance from my house, and my check-in time for surgery was 5:00am. My family and I decided to check into a hotel next to the hospital the night before the surgery. My parents kept my daughter in their room so my husband and I could be alone. It was the strangest, most special, most difficult night of my married life. I was so afraid of how my husband and our relationship might change because of the conspicuous absence of "the twins."

I was never a big fan of how God designed my body, but I was always proud of my chest. It was the one thing about me I thought was just right. My husband had always assured me he had no complaints either. That night we talked a lot. We talked about reconstruction being a possibility in the future, but we didn't know how long it would be. We talked about what type of implants I might want. Tim put in a vote that night for filling them with processed cheese spread. He said it would bring a whole new dimension to eating crackers in bed. I love my crazy husband, and that night he told me again that he loved *me*, not my figure or lack of it. He loved me. That's what gave me the strength to get up the next morning.

When the surgery was over and I woke up in recovery, the first thing I did was look down. Since I was in fifth grade I have been no less than a C cup. I hadn't had a clear view of my abdomen from above for over 25 years. The first thing I noticed was how huge my stomach looked. I mean, I looked fat; really fat. Of course, I didn't go into surgery looking like a runway model, but I didn't remember having such a wide girth. Then I looked at my chest. Even with the bandages it was flat, and I mean *flat*. The surgeons had been so thorough, and rightfully so, that I was left with reverse cleavage. What I mean by that is all the muscle and tissue was gone down to the bone, and my sternum actually protruded slightly. My upper chest looked like a photo from Auschwitz. Now why couldn't they have done that with my belly and hips?

I'd like to tell you I took it all in stride. I'd like to say I laughed it off. I'd like to, but it wouldn't be right to start lying now. I cried. The nurses thought I was in pain, but they mistook where the hurt was located. No amount of Morphine® was going to take care of this one. I think that was my real wake-up call. Up to that moment it could all still have been unreal. I could maintain denial. I didn't feel sick even though medical imaging and blood work said otherwise. But when I looked down, there was no going back, no denying it anymore. I had breast cancer, and just because the boobs were gone didn't mean it was over.

It was a few days before I could bring myself to look at my whole body in a mirror. That was a shock. I couldn't decide what I looked like. It was a toss up between a bowling pin and a penguin. Even at my heaviest weight, my body had always been balanced. Now my bottom half looked bigger than it had ever been because there was nothing up top to off-set it. It was awful. I felt completely disfigured, and every time I walked past a mirror I was reminded of it. There was no getting away from it. If I thought having eye contact with people before was difficult, now it was downright impossible!

The place all this had the largest impact was in my marriage. After I had healed from surgery, there was still no denying I was now shaped like a very bald penguin, and I felt uglier than that little duckling of story book fame had ever imagined. I don't know how it works for other people. I'm sure I'm the only one like this, but when I feel ugly, I automatically assume that is how the rest of the world sees me. I felt hideous, and I was certain my husband felt the same way. Of course, he told me didn't, but he was supposed to say that, wasn't he? Isn't that all part of being the supportive husband?

I found it almost impossible to receive any truth in his reassurances. I didn't want him near me because I was certain I was repulsive to him and that he was faking anything he felt when it came to intimacy. What had once been a key part of our physical relationship was now a no-fly zone because it was just so awkward. Awkward is not a good word when talking about being intimate with someone you've been married to for almost fifteen years.

People look at me and tell me how inspirational I am. The real hero is my husband. He patiently loved me through every stupid lie I told myself, and I know at times it had to be very lonely for him. But we came through it, and our marriage is more precious to us now than it could ever have been if God had not taken us to this place. My husband taught me to see myself differently. God used him to show me what was and is truly beautiful about myself.

It's not easy to look in the mirror at multiple scars across your chest, your lower body bloating from steroids, and a hair-do getting ready to fall out and say, "I will praise You for I am fearfully and wonderfully made (Psalm 139:14)." He says He has, "endowed me with splendor (Isaiah 55:5)." Yeah, right. I didn't see anything splendid or wonderful in that mirror. In fact, I avoided all mirrors.

It was in a moment such as that when I had to ask God for the ability to see myself as He sees me. I knew that when He looked at me, He saw His glory, manifested in the body of His Son, in-dwelt in me. So then I stopped looking at my reflection and started looking at Christ's.

My scars would never compare. My losses would never measure up. I saw His head, full of holes around the hairline. I saw His chest with a hole in His side, long strips of missing flesh where the whip wrapped around His body. When I looked in His eyes, my missing eyelashes were replaced with a love so deep, I will never be able to completely fathom. Suddenly I saw that my value is not in my appearance, in my abilities, in my words, or in my mere existence. My value is less than inconsequential. God discarded it and replaced it with His Son's.

So take a closer look in the mirror. Now do you see your splendor? Now do you see the beautiful fearfulness of your being? Beauty fades, flowers whither, hair falls out, things sag, and parts grow wider rather than taller. But the glory of the Lord, *the glory of the Lord*, desires to dwell in you and endow you with an everlasting splendor.

Did that make it easier to undress or look in the mirror or go shopping? Not always, but each day I was alive was a day I was alive, and that is what eventually broke through to me. The doctors can cut away at the body, but they can't touch the part that makes each individual wonderfully unique and splendid. That's definitely got to go on the good list!

Prosthesis Mishaps

The female anatomy has long been a source of giggles for the pre-teen boy. Let's face it, even grown men giggle about it. That's okay. I understand. Dealing with prosthetic breasts gave me the giggles, too. Yes, folks, the greatest source for laughter during and after breast cancer has to be, hands down, the fake boobies. If you can't laugh at yourself, this will be your worst nightmare. If you make a choice, like I have, to find God's humor in every day life, you are in for a treat here.

It starts shortly after surgery when you are issued your first set of "prosthesis." When I heard this term, I thought the cancer society volunteer was confused. I wasn't missing a limb. It turns out that everything fake that replaces something that used to be real on your body is considered a prosthetic. Okay ... I think.

My first set of prosthesis was made of cotton. They were small, and I mean small, cotton pillows sewn in a wedge shape that could be inserted in a bra that was bigger and scarier looking than anything that ever fell out of my grand-mother's laundry basket. The purpose is to give you a little shape while you're still healing from surgery. The bra, while very large, is light and actually comfort-able. The cotton boobs are soft and have no weight to them. That's nice because you're still healing from a giant gash in your chest where some crazy doctor scooped out half your body. There is one small problem, though. Things that weigh less are affected less by gravity.

This point was driven home not long after I started wearing them. I substi-tuted one day at the high school and was constantly writing things on the board. Every time I raised my arm, my entire bra, boob inserts included, would ride up to my neck. This happens to everyone to a certain extent, but think about it. Without something attached to my body to keep the clothes down, my shirt and inflated bra were always riding up. What made it worse was that it didn't weigh enough to come back down on its own. It's one thing to keep pulling your shirt tail down in a crowd. It's quite another to find a way to discreetly reseat your boobs every time you lift your hand.

So, here I was in a classroom of high school students faced with a most inter-esting choice. Do I grab the cotton things and yank them down, or do I just leave them sitting on my collar bone and hope no one notices? My solution was frequent trips to the bathroom. The students didn't find out about my prosthetic woes, but by the end of the day, I'm sure they were convinced I had an incontinence problem.

Even when I got my "real" fake boobs I was told not to wear them swimming, especially in the salt-water of the ocean. "Just use your cotton ones." Guess what? Cotton floats. You need lots and lots of safety pins. Of course, you could do what I did. Go to the beach and play in the waves. It won't be long before someone is writing home on a postcard about the bald, penguin-shaped lady they saw in the ocean shouting to her husband, "Quick, grab my boobs! They're floating out to sea!"

If you are looking for humor, you don't have to look any further than the process of shopping for those "real" fake boobs. It's much more fun if you take someone with you. I took my best friend. We walked into a specialty shop and a very nice lady took us to a changing room. I had to strip to the waist while the lady brought in a half dozen boxes of prosthesis and bras. We were there a half hour while she shoved one set after another into the bra and then asked my opinion.

My friend and I kept comparing size, shape, and texture. It was wild! We couldn't stop laughing. "Well, that one is a little rounder than this one." "This one is squishier, but it doesn't jiggle as much as that one." I knew better than to take my husband. He would have been seriously overloaded!

I finally settled on a pair, but, of course, they only had the left one in stock. So I walked out with a new left boob and a loaner boob for the right side. I confess it felt good walking around. It was the first time I had felt anything close to normal since my surgery. I knew they weren't real, but they looked real, and I looked normal when I caught my reflection. I had several ladies ask if I would give them my set when I finished with them. The hard part was not to grope them all the time. They felt so real! People wonder but are too polite to ask.

Sometimes they can get you into trouble. At the risk of sounding like a famous Dustin Hoffman character, I would like to state here and now that I believe I am an excellent driver. I am much more aware of the road than my husband is. I don't scare people nearly as much as he does when I drive. However, my driving record is much more spotted than Tim's. I've never been in a serious accident, but I've had more than one fender bumping incident. My most recent was the year after my mastectomies, and it really wasn't my fault. I blame it on the boobs.

As you have probably surmised by now, I'm very open about how I feel and what I'm experiencing. I welcome questions and love to answer them. In my work with teenagers I think it is very important to encourage questions, and teenage girls always had a lot of questions about my prosthesis.

It was a Sunday afternoon and a few girls and I had some time to kill before evening church services so I drove them to a local coffee shop. While there and on the way back, the conversation turned to my cancer and my prosthetics. The girls were curious and fascinated but afraid to ask too much and be impolite. I'm a pretty up front kind of girl, so to put them at ease, I slipped one boob out and passed it around the car. The girls were amazed at how real it felt and the weight of it. Most importantly, the act of being so open with them made them comfortable with my disease and recovery.

Once the boob had made the rounds in the car it was returned to me, and I attempted to reload it into my bra. You may have seen people driving and talking on a cell phone, driving and eating, and even driving and applying make-up, but driving and reloading a breast prosthetic takes driving to a whole new level. I didn't pass the test. I didn't see the guy's brake lights until it was too late. I was able to stop enough so that we only bumped him instead of really hitting him. Still, there I sat with a car full of young Christian girls less than a mile from the church with a fake boob in my hand. I could just picture it: "Well, officer, you see what happened was … well … I was trying to reload and … want to see it?" Fortunately I was able to quickly slip the prosthetic into its rightful place, and the other driver graciously dismissed the whole matter.

I never did explain to him why I wasn't really watching like I should have been. While it's easy to be open with women about the particulars, a face-to-face explanation with a man I had never met just didn't seem prudent at the time. Of course, when we got back to church the first thing the girls did was run to their parents and friends shouting, "We hit a car with Mrs. Cara's boob!" Their version sounds a lot more interesting, doesn't it?

I'm proud to say my fake boobs have even won awards. I started teaching high school just a few months after I finished chemo. I was very honest with my students about my medical condition. Two of my girls had to do a major project for a club, and they chose to do a study and presentation on breast cancer. When it came time to go to regional competition, I offered to send a prosthetic with them. They were ecstatic, and I couldn't think of a better reason to be lopsided for a weekend.

The girls had worked very hard, and it paid off because they were chosen to go to the state level competition. The next month when the date rolled around they asked if they could borrow my boob again. (I think I need to add that to the list of things you never expect to be asked.) I didn't want to create sibling rivalry in my set so this time I sent the other boob. I figured that way they could swap stories in the drawer overnight. It could be a new conversation topic for them. Yes, I know, fake boobs don't talk, but if they could ...

One thing you never think about is what to do with the boobs when you're done with them. After reconstruction I certainly didn't need them anymore, but I was hesitant to throw them away. First of all, they had cost quite a bit of money, and it didn't seem right to just toss them. Mostly though, they were a crutch, like keeping your big clothes after you lose a lot of weight. Yes, I don't need them now, but I might later and then where would I be? It amused and saddened me at how hard it was to let go of those silly things. They sat buried in a drawer for almost two years. I'd think about getting rid of them, but I just couldn't.

I came up with several "good" reasons to hang on to them. I might need them for a theatre costume. I could loan them to a teenage girl for her prom dress. Maybe I could use them for doorstops? I knew it was an issue of faith. It was like I was telling God I trusted Him but not completely. Just in case He screwed it up, I wanted a backup plan.

God hates backup plans, and I could see that it really was ridiculous. God kept telling me He had brought me this far, and it was He who would carry me farther, not those oddly shaped pieces of plastic. I had to give them up, but I still couldn't throw them away. A few phone calls revealed that some prosthetics can be returned or donated for ladies who can't afford them. Mine were pretty well worn so I decided to laugh; make a joke out of it like I had everything else. The boobs are now in the possession of my best friend. We are going to have them encased and give them to my husband. The small inscription on the frame will read, "In case of emergency, break glass."

Sometimes you can't help but laugh at it all. Admit it. Life can be funny and even in the midst of crisis, God will always provide a moment for a smile. It's an opportunity to breathe during all the stress. Trust me; when you're treading water for your life and you feel like you keep going under, you need every breath you can get. So go ahead and giggle. You'll be better for it.

Reconstruction

In 2005, I decided to pursue reconstructive surgery. Many women are very content with a prosthetic device. For me it continued to be a struggle emotionally. I just never felt complete. Maybe that was a failure on my part, but I couldn't change how I felt. I've never seen other mastectomy patients as incomplete; it was just an image I projected onto myself. I was in my mid 30s, and I just couldn't face the next 40 plus years being shaped like a bowling pin.

If I thought the entire prosthesis element was funny, then reconstruction could provide me with enough comic material to start a night club act. The first step is to find a good plastic surgeon. This can be tricky. It's really frowned upon when you walk up to strangers and say, "I love your breasts. Where did you have them done?" Fortunately, oncologists and gynecologists can make referrals without you having to do all the embarrassing survey work yourself.

There are several different ways to reconstruct the breast. They all involve moving muscle tissue and stretching skin. If reconstruction is what you want, be sure to do your research before you go in. That way you have questions already prepared. My plastic surgeon informed me that because of my physical condition and medical history, there was really only one good way for me to go. The plan was to cut the latissimus muscles in my back, bring them around to the front under my skin, tack them down and place implants beneath them. Sounds simple enough, doesn't it? The procedure was predicted to take eight or more hours with two surgeons working simultaneously, one on each side.

The really interesting part for me was when we had to discuss the type of implant I wanted; saline versus silicone. There are pros and cons for each. Silicone has lost its bad reputation lately and is a very safe option, and they do feel more realistic. Saline is just that, the same type of fluid your body already uses so if you have a blowout, it's not a big deal. No internal cleanup is necessary. Of course, they feel slightly different. How do I know how they feel? The doctor handed me one of each to compare. Let me tell you, you haven't lived until you're sitting in a plastic surgeon's office comparing breast implants. I really toyed with the thought of asking for a third and making an attempt at juggling.

Even funnier was when my husband went with me to the second appointment. I figured he would be feeling them more than me, and I wanted his input. I've never seen Tim embarrassed, but when the doctor offered him my juggling toys he mumbled a quick, "No, thank you," with a very red face. Apparently this must happen a lot because the doctor made a point of leaving the implants on the counter next to Tim and excusing himself from the room for a moment. No sooner had the door clicked closed than my husband was, shall we say, comparing apples and oranges. Even funnier was how fast he dropped them as soon as the door began to open again a few minutes later. I don't know if it was his lightning quick reflexes or the sheepish grin, but I laughed so hard, I cried.

One lesson I've learned is to be prepared for the consequences when you tell God that you trust Him. I had worked so hard to be organized and make sure everything was in order for my surgery. I double checked the dates, planned ahead at school, prepared additional lesson plans, trained a sub, and deep cleaned the house. I'd even arranged for friends to come and take down all the Christmas decorations since I wouldn't be able to raise my arms, much less carry all the boxes back up to the attic. Yep, everything was going great.

I wasn't the least bit concerned about the procedures themselves. That thought struck me hard the Sunday before the surgery. I was so unconcerned I hadn't even prayed about it. I began to feel guilty. Was my faith so small that I hadn't given this over to God? God, in His deafening, silent way, spoke to me and asked me if I had ever prayed for the sun to come up or the grass to grow, or the seasons to change. No? Why? Because I trusted Him so completely with those things that I just went on my way. My not fretting and praying continuously about my surgeries was a sign that my faith had grown. So I went on my merry way, very proud of myself and my insight.

What's that verse about pride going before … I should have seen it coming. I said, "I trust you, God." And in His loving way, He said, "Oh, yeah? How much?" By Sunday night I had developed a cough. By Monday it was a full-blown chest cold complete with fever. If I was sick, no surgeries. I had been waiting two years. I didn't want to wait any longer. Everything was ready for now. "Do you still trust Me?" *Yes, Lord, and I'm on the way to the doctor's office right now!* One sinus cocktail shot and ten hours of sleep and all the cold symptoms were gone by Tuesday. The surgery was back on schedule; that is, until the phone call came.

I had planned a total hysterectomy to be done at the same time as my reconstruction; kind of a two-for-one special. One surgeon's office had never been told about the procedure they were scheduled to do, never heard about it! I had 24 hours to get in to see them, to have them completely rearrange their schedule, and to get insurance to approve it. What a nightmare. "Do you still trust Me?" *Yes, Lord, and I'm on the way to the doctor's office right now!* Several phone calls and a lot of prayers later, the surgeries (plural) were a go again. Needless to say, I was emotionally exhausted. Did I mention I was trying to do a month's worth of Christmas shopping in the midst of this medical mayhem?

Then I heard the rest of what God had been waiting to teach me. On Sunday I had trusted Him because *I* had put everything in order. *I* had done everything in my power. I hadn't really needed Him. By Monday, everything was out of my hands. I mean, it was way out of my hands, and it only got farther out of my hands from there. That is where the real faith kicked in. How willing was I to trust God when I was completely out of control? The answer? More than I thought and much less than God wanted. Yes sir, I learned quite a bit about telling God I trust Him. I won't hesitate to tell Him again, but next time, I'll certainly try not to be as surprised when He puts it to the test.

I must say, I felt different after my surgeries. I'll never forget the first alert moment I had in the recovery room. The first thing I did was look down. For two years all I had seen was a protruding sternum. This time, even with the bandages, I saw cleavage. I didn't cry; I wept, and I kept whispering, "Thank You." I can say all the right things about value coming from God. Oh, I can talk the talk, but at the end of the day, I'm just as human as the next girl. Those implants made all the difference in how I felt about myself. My clothes fit right again, my body was balanced, and I didn't hate catching a glimpse of myself in the mirror coming out of the shower. Yes, it's shallow. Yes, it's vain. But it's the truth.

Because of the size of breast I wanted and needed for my body size, my skin had to be stretched. This meant I was given temporary implants. Just beneath the surface of the skin was a small valve like on an IV tube. Every two weeks I would go to the doctor. He would take a needle large enough to make an elephant quiver and fill it with saline. He would then inject the saline into the implant, thereby slighting increasing its size and stretching the skin to gradually make room for the permanent implant. It was a simple procedure and didn't hurt a bit since all sensation in my chest region had been destroyed by the two surgeries. However, there are few things I wasn't prepared for with reconstruction surgery.

I knew that a flap of skin would be removed from each side of my back to create a pocket for the implants. What I didn't know was that I have back hair. How do I know this? It's now in front. Thankfully, I'm not manly in that way, but it's there. Should I count back hair as chest hair? Or is it "breast hair?" I don't know.

The whole thing is a little confusing to me. The bigger question is whether to shave it or wax it because I draw the line at chest/breast hair.

Another thing that threw me for a loop was the muscle spasms. Two muscles were moved from my back to my front. Now I do not have the ability to do the breast stroke. Don't you love the irony? I gave up the breast stroke for breasts! It makes me giggle. Anyway, with those muscles gone, the other muscles in my back have had to pick up the slack. Everyone has a new job description, and they frequently argue over them. These little muscle debates are very painful because you can't stretch out the cramps and spasms very well.

Something truly fascinating also happened with the newly relocated muscles. The one on my right breast would spasm without warning or provocation. Out of nowhere my right breast would begin to boogie like it was Saturday night. It was very noticeable. This made teaching even more of an adventure. My students knew I had taken time off for reconstruction. When I came back from sick leave, it was hilariously sweet how many of my male students wouldn't even look in my general direction for fear of offending me. I finally got them past that so I could make eye contact, and now my chest is fluttering so much, I contemplated tattooing a butterfly or hula girl on it. It was so hysterical. The spasm came under control after a few months, but to this day I don't shiver when I'm cold; my boobies dance.

I have a beautiful daughter. She is truly a gift from God. She's one of those girls who will always be naturally slender, with willowy limbs. She looks cute in anything she tries on. Since she was a baby, people have been telling her how pretty she is, and they are right; however, I've tried to teach her that beauty comes from within. Ask her what makes you pretty, and she'll repeat what I've repeated to her almost every day of her life. Loving Jesus is what makes you pretty. Whether your breasts are natural, cotton, plastic, saline, or silicone, they are not the source of your beauty. You must understand this. Reconstruction will not solve your bad self image. You must get in touch with the truth that God sees your beauty because He sees His workmanship in you. The world does not define your value. God does.

Life after Cancer

It Can't Be the Way It Was

Now to answer the question of the ages: Is there life after cancer? *Absolutely!* It's a wonderful life, too, but it will be different than the life you have known. The beautiful thing about life is that it is on-going and therefore produces change. If you don't like it, stop living. Otherwise buckle your seatbelt and enjoy the ride.

Remember when you were an adolescent? Adolescents go through the process of asking: Who am I? How do I deal with life? What do I really believe? How do I feel about myself? How do I feel about other people? It's a self-exploration, self-defining period in life. When you go through cancer, you have to go through that all over again, whether it's one time or fifteen.

I wasn't crazy about adolescence the first time. Do you know many people who were? It can be more than frustrating to feel like you are back there again. The person you were before the cancer and the person you are after are not the same; not physically, mentally, emotionally, or spiritually. I know that sounds ridiculously simple, but it's more profound than you might realize. The body you had before cancer is not the body you have now. You must accept that.

After cancer things can never be the way they were. From here on out every time you don't feel 100% well, you will wonder if the cancer is back. With every strange bump, every unusual mole, every unexplained headache you will immediately ask yourself, "Is it back?" You see, cancer is never over even after the chemo. Even though it is no longer a part of you, it is still a *part* of you.

I expected the mental changes. I think I was a little more surprised by the physical changes. I think I just assumed that, once chemo was over, everything in my body would go back to normal. Let me just tell you now, give up on that pipe dream, and learn to embrace weirdness. I've been sick so many times in my life with cancer that it has really come to define who I am. Sometimes it's almost as though I have Munchausen's Syndrome. I don't rightly know who I am when I'm well.

One thing that happened with the first round of chemo was major depression. No one warned me this might happen and what it might look like, so it took several years to finally admit the problem and treat it. Chemo has left me chemically unbalanced and, therefore, much more prone to depression. I have to really keep on eye on it. In my own head, it took a long time for me to get past the stigma of taking anti-depressants. Now I embrace them as a helpful tool, and my family loves my "happy pills."

After the last chemo, I didn't think I would ever get my brain back. My husband would insert several comments here, but since I'm the author I'll just move on. Loss of ability to focus, concentrate, and remember is common with chemo, and it usually goes away within a few months of stopping the medication. However, it can have a cumulative effect which is what happened in my case. I'll never be the sharpest tack in the box again. I tell my kids I've done too many drugs and fried my brain. I love messing with their heads and watching them try to figure out if I'm kidding or truly a recovering addict.

Actually, the truth is I *am* a recovering addict. The depression brought on by chemo in my teen years led into alcohol abuse in my twenties. It took my father finding a trash bag full of my beer bottles to make me stop cold turkey. I've also recently admitted to myself and others that my use of pain medication needs to be monitored closely. Having so many surgeries and migraines in my life, I have a high tolerance to pain medication. It takes a lot to work, and it has to be really strong. Tylenol® just doesn't cut it. I asked my doctor to make a note in my file that pain meds are to be given only in written form, only a few at a time, and the scrip is to be handed to my husband, not me. Cancer has taught me that even if I can't control something, I don't have to let it control me.

In my early 30s I started feeling exhausted all the time. I couldn't pinpoint any one thing that was wrong, I just didn't feel right. If you've had cancer, you know what I mean. After struggling with it for awhile, I went to the doctor for a general workup. It turns out there was nothing medically wrong, which made no sense to me because I kept feeling bad.

My doctor tried to explain it this way. With all my body has been through, physically I'm 20 years older than my actual age. I didn't know if that was supposed to make me feel better or worse. I guess I should look on the bright side. I may not be doing great for 40, but if I get to add 20 years I'm rocking out at 60!

Whether I like it or not, my body has been forced to slow down. I need to slow down with it which requires some planning on my part. I have to choose my activities much more carefully. I've learned the very important word "no" and learned to not feel guilty when I use it. I simply can't do everything, and it's foolish to expect that of myself. If people don't understand, I'll try to explain, but it's not really my problem if they don't get it. I have to take care of myself for my sake and the sake of my family.

I'm a busy lady so I actually have to calendar down time for myself. I have to look at how much time I leave myself between major projects. Mental work wears me out on a physical level, and stress, although a driving force in my life, can wear me down as well. I have to allow for those things. If I've got a major play going on at school, I know that I can't be doing a lot of other projects during that time. I need down time between trips, whereas before I could travel twelve weeks at a time without a break.

One thing I fear is hard for people to really understand is how easily I get sick and how much harder the minor illnesses hit me. Because my immune system is weakened, I get sick more easily. A simple cold knocks me out, and it takes me longer to recover. My body has to work so hard to overcome the virus or infection that it adds an extra layer of exhaustion to the illness.

It takes longer to heal. I've had to learn to adjust for this and give my body the time it needs. Pushing myself to heal at the normal speed only makes the situation worse and prolongs recovery. This is especially true for any surgeries. I seriously misjudged the recovery time on my hysterectomy and reconstruction. I went back to teaching after the prescribed six weeks, but it took months for me to really get back to where I was before the surgery.

My life has been so unique, I wouldn't know a normal life if it walked up and bit me on the nose. But, I can tell you the life I live now is full and satisfying. Don't get me wrong. It has its frustrations. Honestly, though, cancer hasn't made my life harder; different, maybe, but not harder. Of course, being different is my specialty. I thrive on being the oddball. After all, everybody has to have their niche.

Survivor's Guilt

On April 19, 1994, I was awakened by the repercussions of an explosion that shook our world. I lived in Oklahoma City, Oklahoma. Over the next days and months I was part of a community trying to recover from an atrocity committed by one of our own countrymen. As the city and state went through the grieving process, a term came up over and over again that gave a name and definition to another issue with which I had struggled since I was first recovered from cancer: survivor's guilt.

Simply put, survivor's guilt wrestles with the question, "Why did I survive and he didn't?" It says things like, "She was so much younger than I." "He had children and I don't. Why didn't he get to live?" "They had so much more to offer the world than I do." I am not a psychologist so I am not able to explain it all to you. I can only tell you how it feels in my life.

Not everyone beats cancer the way God allowed me to. The hardest thing in the world for me is hearing that someone I know has been given a terminal diagnosis. It's happened four times with close friends, people who were significant in my life or my husband's life. One would think I would be there all the time for them, ready with all kinds of advice, but the truth is, I almost avoid the situation. It's survivor's guilt. *Why are they dying whereas I get to live? He only had cancer once, and he's not going to make it. Why did God choose me over him?*

These thoughts paralyze my ability to bring comfort because I am certain that the diagnosed and his family are thinking the same thing. I feel like if I show up to visit I am throwing my health in their face. *Yep, too bad about you, but hey, at least I came out okay.* I know in my head that this is untrue, but the emotion of it is still very incapacitating.

My dear friend, Larry, was diagnosed with cancer. He fought hard for an exceptionally long time, but he would always tell me what an inspiration I was to him. You can't imagine how hard that was to hear. In some ways it only made me feel worse. Here was a man refusing to stop living his life until the moment God took him home, and he was building me up.

When my youth minister and spiritual mentor, Jerry Solomon, was dying from pancreatic cancer, he asked me, "How do you do this?" I didn't know. I had no answers. I knew how to survive cancer, but I didn't know how to die from it. I still see Larry and Jerry's families from time to time even though I've moved away, but it's hard. For the longest time, a part of me feared that they would be bitter toward me because I made it and their loved one didn't. I know it's silly, but it was how I felt. I did a lot of praying about it. I know God has given me a ministry to cancer patients, and I can't let false messages of survivor's guilt get in the way. So how did I learn to deal with it? God sent Gray.

Gray was a student of mine. By the time he came to me he had already been fighting brain cancer for several years. Gray was an amazing kid. The first time I met him, my heart went out to him because I *knew* what it was like to be kid and have cancer. I reached out to him immediately because I wanted him and his family to know there was one person in the school who really got it; all of it. Even though he wasn't enrolled in my classes that first year, my room was his rest haven. The next year, when he was a sophomore, Gray was actually my student in two classes.

Gray had a truly wonderful, warped sense of humor. We got along great, and we had many wonderful talks. When you have to constantly define medical terms to everyone, in every conversation, you get to the point where you just stop talking because it's too much effort. Gray and I spoke the same language. I like to think it made it easier for him to know that he could walk into my room and say, "My counts are low," and I would immediately know how he felt and how much he could contribute for the day.

I watched Gray fight cancer every day until the bitter end. I couldn't hide from him out of my own guilt. He was there in front of me every day, and I had to find a way to get past myself. It wasn't easy. Each day we would see him get weaker. He joked less, and I could tell his pain was getting worse; but he refused to stop coming to school. It was his way of not letting cancer win. My students and I watched his courage and his nobility, and it changed us.

Shortly before he died, my class made a request. With the permission and support of our principal, we named our school mascot, the Horn Lake High School eagle, Gray. One of my students put it best when she told Gray that a mascot was supposed to represent a hero, and he was our hero. The funeral was difficult for everyone. Gray was loved by so many, but I sat there fighting my own personal demons. I watched his parents and his younger brothers and thought, *here was a kid who had his whole life in front of him. Why would God choose to take him and leave me?* There were no answers.

It's still hard. I feel guilty every time I see Gray's mother. Does she want to talk about Gray? Does she not want to talk about Gray? Does it bother her that

I'm still alive and her son isn't? I don't know. I'm still working through this one. You see, that's the thing about cancer never being over. I'll be working through the emotional trauma of it for the rest of my life. Still, I think that's probably a good thing. Everyone has something they are working through. It's normal, and it probably won't ever go away completely. In some ways I don't want it to. If the guilt went away, I'm afraid that would mean I just don't care. I think the guilt is natural; I just can't let it direct my choices.

When my mom called me about a friend of ours, Carr, who was terminal, I really hesitated to contact him. I mean, what do you say? Sorry you're dying? I knew that was the guilt talking. I actually tried to call a couple of times but never made contact. So I wrote a long letter. I told him everything I felt about him, what an impact he had made in my life, and what a legacy I felt he was leaving. I told him how the world was a better place because of him.

The final lesson for me of learning how to deal with the guilt of not being dead is still being taught by a sweet lady in my church, Doris. She and her husband, Jim, were key people in my husband's early ministry and have continued to be instrumental at several significant turns in our life. Jim was diagnosed with pancreatic cancer and passed away in 2006. Doris continues to be an active member of our church. I can't hide from her or choose to avoid her because of my fear. Bless her heart, Doris won't let me. Doris has answered some of my questions without me even asking. She lets me know when she wants to talk about Jim by bringing him up. Most of the time, we just have normal conversations. Pretty profound, isn't it? Doris and I are just people who loved Jim and miss him. No guilt involved.

Guilt implies that somehow I'm responsible for what happened. People are found guilty of crimes. I'm guilty of not meeting a work deadline. I had nothing to do with Larry, Jerry, Gray, Carr, or Jim dying from cancer. The guilt there is misplaced. It wasn't my fault, and it certainly wasn't my choice. I wouldn't wish cancer on my worst enemy.

Having said all that, the next time someone I love gets a diagnosis, I'll probably still feel guilty. The difference is that I've learned not to let the guilt paralyze me, not to let it isolate me. God has brought me through for a reason. I believe the reason is to express what He has taught and is teaching me through all the cancers. To stop doing what He has left me here to do would be a crime of which I never want God to find me guilty.

Your "New Family"

The day I was diagnosed with cancer for the first time was the day I gained a new family. It includes every doctor that will ever treat me, every nurse in every treatment room, every woman who sports a pink ribbon, and every person whose life has been personally touched by cancer. Sometimes I know them by what they are wearing or how they style their hair (or lack of it). Sometimes we realize we are kindred spirit through conversation. We speak the same language.

With us there is no need to define terms. There is no need to delineate possible side effects. We compare notes on which tests we hated the most and who can do the best blood draw on tricky veins. We share our successes and carry each others' pain in our own hearts. Just like a family, some pass before us. My first oncologist, Dr. Lloyd Kitchens, passed away from Crohn's Disease just a few years after my 20-year Hodgkin's disease-free milestone. In this special family it was like losing a parent. I suppose some small part of me never thought I would outlive the man who saved my life.

Cancer is scary. Strike that. It's terrifying, but this family knows it. They don't just say, "I know how you feel." They really do know. They've been there. They understand every needle stick, every MRI, every side effect, and every surgery. Even the doctors and nurses get it. The medical personnel in the oncology field are a special breed. I have found in them an amazing ability to immediately trust that the patient knows what he's talking about. Are you scared? Sure you are. Admit it. Are you alone? Never. This is no surprise to God. He knew it would happen, and He's standing right beside you. To prove it He's surrounding you with other people who can physically hug you on His behalf. They can hold your hand and answer your questions. Most important, you can pick up the phone at 2:00am when you can't sleep, and they listen as you pour out your heart. Don't believe me? Look around the room the next time you go in to see your doctor.

Cancer is a battle, and no one should fight a battle alone. Ask for help. Call for reinforcements. Personally, I didn't need to talk to a cancer volunteer. I had my family. Maybe you do. Contact the American Cancer Society and tell them. No one will help you if they don't know you need it. This is a family and, just like my biological family, my life would be incomplete without them.

How Others Can Help

So You Want to Help

When you find out someone is in need, you want to help. It's human nature. We are hard wired to nurture and show compassion. It's because we're made in the image of God. What can present a challenge is knowing how to express those emotions, especially when the situation seems so devastating. I will say this: it is much easier for me to be the sick one than the caregiver. I've done cancer more often. I'm an old pro at how to handle the surgeries and treatments. That's because it's about me, and I know what I want and how I feel.

It's a little bit harder when it's someone else. Just because I felt a certain way doesn't mean they will share that sentiment. I'm not a mind reader so I've learned to just come out and ask. I can't help if I don't know what they need. They may not know how to tell me, so communication is the key. Here are some tips I've picked up along the way.

If your friend, let's call him Joe, is diagnosed and you want to know how he is doing, don't ask Joe's friends and family. Ask Joe. Call him up. If he can't talk, he'll have someone talk for him, but go straight to him with your questions. This communicates several things. First of all, Joe knows you're asking about him. He knows you care.

Second, you are letting him know you want to know specifics. You want him to be able to talk details, and you want to learn what he is learning. Trusting someone besides Joe to relay his medical updates can get really out of hand. We've all played that game where you start a sentence and repeat it down the line to the end. Information warps as it travels. It's a universal fact.

I missed one day of teaching with a migraine. I made a late night trip to the emergency room and called a friend so someone would know what was going on. By the end of the following afternoon, my students were calling my cell phone because they heard I was dying. One had heard I was already dead! Funny as it seems, give your friend the respect he deserves by asking him directly.

As a teen, one sweet little lady would call every day and ask my mother for an update. Many days there was nothing new to report, but she was faithful in her calling. I later learned that each day when she hung up the phone she immediately prayed for me based on what she had just been told. I knew she cared. Your friend needs to know that, too.

Insist on helping the patient and their family. Take the initiative. The next section gives several suggestions, but the key is being specific. Make them list needs they have and see which one you can meet. Grocery run? Return a library book? Sit with me? Help them know how you can help them by making them be specific. More importantly, if you say you are going to help, *follow through!*

Cancer is a life-changing disappointment. It shatters the myth that each person works so hard to carry. You know the one: I will live a long, healthy life and die old, in my sleep in my own bed. It may still happen, but the reality is now clear that it's not a guarantee. That's a pretty big let down. Don't be part of the let down. If you can't help, don't offer. That's okay. Honestly, everyone wants to help, but a family can only consume so many casseroles from neighbors before you have to draw the line. Just say what you mean and do what you say. Actually that's not a bad rule for life in general.

Even if you can't drive, or cook, or whatever, everyone is capable of doing one thing: praying. Pray and pass the name along to someone else who you know will pray.

When I was 13 and recovering from surgery, my father took his youth choir on a trip. In each church where they sang, he asked the congregation to pray for me. Over the next few months, I got over one hundred letters of prayer from across the South. It completely overwhelmed me that total strangers were praying for me.

This last time I had cancer I, of course, told my friends. One day, when I was feeling particularly ugly, small, and alone, God revealed something to me: the whole world was praying for me. I had friends all across the United States reading my e-mails. I had friends and acquaintances in Germany and Portugal who were praying for me along with their churches. I could even name people in the African bush who knew my name and were lifting me up in prayer in their little village church.

I don't say all that to brag about how significant I am. On the contrary, God used it to show me that though I may be small, I am a crucial part in His tapestry. Each of us alone is insignificant in what we can accomplish, but God tells us that much prayer accomplishes much. So pray, and don't stop praying. Just because you don't see answers, or the answers you want, doesn't mean you aren't accomplishing anything. Your loved one knows you care and that soothes their spirit. You grow closer to God as you talk with Him, and God will answer prayer. I know He does.

Ideas for Helping

One of the casualties of cancer tends to be relationships. While it is scary to be the one with the diagnosis, it is also scary to the well-meaning family and friends who want to help but don't know how. People who aren't sure what to say or what to do will often say or do nothing. It doesn't have to be that way. Here are a few of the "helpful hints" I have experienced in my own journey through cancer. Choose one. Choose all, but please choose.

When someone is cut off by illness, it's important that friends find a way to stay in touch. Often times, patients cannot go to the places they once went for fear of getting an infection. Their whole social structure is radically changed. Yet, they still have the same need for closeness, friendship, and fun. In this day and age, there are many ways to stay in touch.

At one point in high school, I was in the hospital for over three weeks. One day, a friend took a camera to church and took about fifty pictures of all the people there: my friends being silly, my teachers waving hello, and even the children's choir I helped with blew me kisses. Each picture was glued in a spiral notebook followed by page after page of notes from my friends. That notebook was such a blessing. It stayed in a drawer by my bed, and when I was hurting or depressed, I would pull it out and draw strength from the love it represented.

The world of computers and digital technology has opened a whole new world of options for helping people feel plugged into life. Now, with the help of inexpensive digital cameras, friends can set up entire websites complete with images to keep the patient connected, and e-mail is only a mouse-click away.

Ask for specific ways you can help. It is as difficult for most people to accept help as it is for them to ask for it, so sometimes you have to take the initiative. Insist on doing something. When I was sick at Christmas time, some friends came over to my house to decorate. All I had to do was point to where I wanted something, and they'd take care of it. A week after Christmas, they were back to help take the decorations down. It was such a blessing.

If the patient asks you how you are, tell the truth. Many times when I was sick, I'd ask someone how they were doing, and I'd get a response such as, "Oh, I'm doing fine. Nothing as bad as what you're going through." How do you know? Your crisis is a crisis to you. Your struggle is a struggle to you. When you don't want to share, it makes it difficult for the patient to focus on anyone else but himself.

As friends, you lean on each other. But if only one person is leaning, eventually you'll both fall down because the load isn't balanced. So when you are asked how you are, give an honest answer without an apology. Let your friend or family member support you just like you want to support them.

There are countless ways to help both patients and their caregivers. The following section provides a few examples. Any gesture, no matter how small you think it may be, is a welcomed message of caring to the one on the receiving end. You may even end up on their "good list."

WHEN THEY ARE IN THE HOSPITAL:

1. Send cards with news of family or friends.

2. Send a care package with such things as reading materials, snacks, Kleenex, CDs, word puzzles, or lotions.

3. Offer to sit and visit with the patient so the family can take a break. You don't have to have great words of wisdom. Your time is a gift. Don't underestimate the value of your presence.

4. Help the caregiver who is at home. This can help put the patient's mind at ease.

5. With some surgeries, such as reconstructive surgery after breast cancer, pillows made specifically for the arms are quite helpful. It takes the pressure off the sutures.

6. When a patient is in isolation, it can be just that; isolating or lonely. Write letters full of news, make a phone call, or make video/audio tapes.

7. Never underestimate the power of a phone call.

8. If the patient's diet isn't restricted, bring them food from their favorite fast food joint. A good chocolate shake can really turn a day around.

9. Bring up a DVD/VCR player and have a movie night. I recommend a good, knee-slapping comedy.

WHEN THEY ARE GOING THROUGH TREATMENT:

1. Offer to drive them.

2. Visit with the patient while he is receiving treatment. This can make the time seem to go quicker.

3. If his hair is falling out, you can wear a hat. If you feel really brave, shave your head.

4. Don't be afraid to call and ask how he is feeling.

5. Provide hard candy and mint gum. They help with mouth sores.

6. Check out some good books from the local library and offer to return them when he is finished.

7. Buy some word or math puzzle books. Chemo drips can be long and boring.

WHEN THEY ARE HOME:

Remember that the caregiver is doing the work of two! Many times, by helping the patient you are also helping the caregiver.

1. Provide meals in disposable containers. It can be helpful if the meal can be frozen to be used at a later time.

2. Take care of the children for a few hours or offer to pick them up from school.

3. If the patient can't drive, take him places or see if you can pick up any items for him while you are out.

4. In the summer, mow the lawn. In the fall, rake the leaves.

5. Light housekeeping can be a big help. It may include a few loads of laundry, dishes, dusting, or vacuuming.

6. Most patients and caregivers appreciate a gift basket of things to help them pamper themselves. These may include lotions, bubble bath, a soft robe, and, of course, chocolate.

7. Buy them some stamps and thank you cards. Offer to write them, dictation style.

8. Call before you go by, but stop in as often as you can.

9. Bring over pictures or video of events the patient misses. Make them feel part of it.

10. I can't say it enough, call and call often. Cancer gets lonely.

Things Caregivers Need to Do for Themselves

In all the attention paid to the person with the diagnosis, it can be easy for you, the caregiver, to be overlooked. This is unfortunate because you are not only caring for the patient but often you are doing the work of two. There are some things that all caregivers can do to help themselves cope with the life-changing events. Educate others on how to help. You have to be specific. While people may be anxious to help, they can't read your mind.

1. Write down a list of specific things you need, when you need it, and the best way for it to be accomplished. For example, if you know Tuesdays are full days and you often don't have time to make dinner, write down, "Dinner—Tuesdays at 5:00pm at the house." The more specific, the better. Be sure to include any dietary restrictions.

2. It doesn't do any good to have a list if you don't allow people to help you. It can be hard to park the pride, I know. But if you have ever received a blessing from helping someone, you know how it feels. Allow others to be blessed by giving to you.

3. Make sure you have some support outside the family. You can look to friends at work, church, in your neighborhood, your health club, or the school. Getting in touch with other people who have overcome cancer in the past can give you a better perspective on things. Talk to people who have been there. Look for support groups. The American Cancer Society is a great place to start.

4. It's important to get away from the illness periodically. You must take time for yourself. There is nothing selfish about this. If you don't, you will be less effective in the care you give to your loved one.

5. Find things to laugh about. You will stay healthier and happier if you can maintain your sense of humor. After being diagnosed with my third cancer, my husband wanted to know if I came with a warranty.

6. Give yourself permission to feel angry or scared or both. These feelings, and others, are very real. They don't go away just because you refuse to acknowledge them. You need to work through them in the same way the patient does. In fact, sharing these feelings with each other can give you both strength and healing. In doing so, you will take your relationship to a whole new level of intimacy; just one more victory you can have over the disease.

7. Keep good notes for insurance purposes. You may want to have your own notebook to keep important papers, track billing and payments, and file correspondence. You never know when you will need that one piece of paper you vaguely remember seeing three months ago. Be sure to date every paper you get.

8. Eat well and get enough sleep.

9. Have a hobby you can participate in periodically to relax.

10. Find an escape place; somewhere that is always accessible to you. It needs to be peaceful and away from your everyday world. It could be the library, local coffee house, or the quiet guest bedroom at your best friend's house. Taking a stroll through the zoo by yourself can be relaxing or sitting on a park bench. You need a place where you can remove yourself from the chaos. You need somewhere you can go where there is no cancer and you can lay down your burden for a short while.

Caregivers have needs, too. Take care of yourself so you can feel good about the care you give.

The One Thing
I Want You to Know

The One Thing
I Want You to Know

There are many things I wanted to pass along in this book: coping with chemotherapy, surviving the sickness, caring for the caregiver, and more. I wanted to express my experience, not as an expert, but as an over-comer. Yes, I am an overcomer, but it is imperative to me that you know the source of that victory.

I do not know why God has chosen to bring me through to the healing side of cancer five times. I *do* know that it is God who has done it. In His great wisdom and love, He has a perfect plan for my life. I will never completely understand it; I'm not God. But I trust His plan, not because He has healed me or may heal me in the future, but because He is God.

I remember vividly the day I came to terms with this truth. I was at a conference called "Passion" in Austin, Texas, and was sitting dead center on the fifteenth row. I heard the heart of God in John Piper's words as he made direct eye contact with me and said, "Do you love God because He's God or because He can cure you of cancer?" The breath went out of me. The man didn't know me, had never met me, but God knew me and His truth pierced my heart.

God taught me that day that He is so much more than just my healer. He is my God; my "I AM." And He has given me so much more than life. He has loved me enough to give me eternal life. I'm afraid of dying, especially of cancer. I think of spending my last days in constant pain with multiple IVs, so high on Morphine® I don't even know my closest family, and dread grips me.

Yes, I'm afraid of the death process, but I'll never fear death. I have a certainty beyond measure that the moment I die I will be in the presence of my Heavenly Father. He will gather me into His arms and all pain, fear, sorrow, and night will be gone forever. I may die of cancer. I may die of laughter on my 92nd birthday. That is not my choice; it is God's. My choice is whether or not to accept God's free gift of a full and wonderful life on earth and eternal life in heaven.

It wasn't a hard choice to make. I realized that I was not perfect; never have been and never will be. My imperfection, my sin, makes it impossible for me to have a relationship with my perfect God. The cost of my sin was eternal separation from God and His love for me.

Everything I had been taught about Jesus was and is true. Jesus and God are one. Jesus, out of love for me, was born as a human baby. He lived a life without defect or mistake. He allowed Himself to be murdered in my place as judgment for my imperfection.

My sin deserved punishment. It's like when you know you've gotten caught by your parents and the punishment is coming. But suddenly, Jesus shows up and says, "I love you so much, I'm going to take your punishment for you." I don't know about you, but my brother never made that offer to me! Jesus did.

It's true that Jesus died. He stopped breathing. His heart stopped beating. Had there been an EEG, He would have been pronounced brain dead. It's true that three days later He came back to life because God is more powerful than anything, even death.

Believing these things to be true, knowing in my heart that these things were facts, I prayed to God. I asked Him to forgive my sin. I asked Him to take control of my life. I confessed with my mouth that Jesus Christ is Lord and believed in my heart that God raised Him from the dead, and I was saved.

No, I wasn't saved from cancer. I may get it again. I wasn't saved from problems, family crisis, or hardship. Life is life. I *was* saved from having to face life on my own. I'm not responsible for solving all my problems. It's not my job to answer all the questions. I have the privilege of leaving all that to God.

I didn't commit intellectual suicide. I merely traded all my doubts, fears, uncertainties, imperfections, and insecurities for a peace that passes all human understanding. I have a peace for today and a bright hope for tomorrow. I know that my life, if I live to 100, is less than a moment in eternity, and no matter how difficult it may seem, it will all disappear that moment I take the nail-scarred hand of Christ.

If you have never talked to God in this way or accepted His gift of eternal life, you can do so by praying a prayer like this:

> *God, I know I am a sinner. I have done things, said things, and thought things that don't please you. I believe that You love me. I believe that Jesus died on the cross to take my punishment and that after three days You raised Him from the dead. Please forgive my sin. From this moment on, I give You my life to do with as You see best. Help me to live for you and enjoy our relationship. I look forward to spending eternity with You. Thank you for saving me and forgiving me. Amen.*

Saying a prayer like this will not accomplish anything on its own. This prayer is only effective if you genuinely understand your own sinfulness and need for salvation, and you believe that Jesus is the only way to having a right relationship with God. If you have prayed this prayer for the first time, allow me to say, "Welcome to God's family!" It is the best decision you could ever make. Be sure to find a Bible-teaching church to help you in your new life with Jesus.

I can't offer you a cure for cancer, but I have found something much more valuable: forgiveness and peace. Isn't that much better? No medicines, no negative side effects, no co-pays and premiums to be met. All you need to do is chose to accept it ... free of charge.

Glossary

Glossary

Crohn's Disease—an inflammatory bowel disease that causes inflammation or ulceration of the digestive tract which can lead to complications and death.

Drip—the continuous, slow introduction of a fluid into a vein of the body using an IV.

EEG—an electroencephalogram; a record of the electrical impulse activity in the brain.

Hodgkin's disease—a type of lymphoma; a cancer of the lymphatic system.

Immuno-Suppression Ward—a section of a hospital used to treat patients whose immune systems are not working effectively due to medical procedures. Extreme measures are taken to maintain a sterile environment.

IV—needle and tubing used to administer an injection directly into a vein.

Latissimus Muscles—a set of muscles in the upper back which allows for over-head arm movement such as that used in swimming with a breast stroke.

Lymph Gland—small, bean-shaped glands that are part of the lymphatic system and are an important part of the immune system. They may be found singly or in groups throughout the body, most dominantly in the neck, armpits, and groin.

Lymphatic System—a network of nodes connected by vessels which together drain fluid and waste products from all the organs and structures of the body. This system is also involved in the production of white blood cells which fight infection.

Metastasis—the transference of malignant or cancerous cells from one part of the body to another by way of the blood or lymphatic vessels.

MRI—magnetic resonance imaging; a test that produces very clear pictures of the body using a large magnet, radio waves, and a computer.

Munchausen's Syndrome—a condition in which a person intentionally fakes, stimulates, worsens, or self-induces an injury or illness for the main purpose of being treated like a medical patient.

Neulasta®—a drug that is prescribed to reduce the risk of infection in some patients receiving chemotherapy. It works by increasing red blood cell production in the bone marrow.

Oncologist—a doctor who specializes in the diagnosis and treatment of cancer.

Papillary Thyroid Cancer—an irregular, solid, or cystic mass that arises from otherwise normal thyroid tissue. It is the most common of all thyroid cancers.

Prognosis—predicting the probable course and outcome of a disease, especially the chances of recovery.

Radioactive Iodine—a liquid medication that is swallowed and absorbed by the thyroid gland. It kills most or all of the tissue of the thyroid gland but does not harm the rest of the body.

Remission—a temporary or permanent decrease or subsidence of manifestations of a disease.

Serotonin—a neurotransmitter produced in the brain that is involved in sleep, depression, memory, and other neurological processes. Low levels can bring on depression and are often caused by chemotherapy.

Steroids—any of various hormones affecting development that are made synthetically, especially for use in medicine. Their specific use in chemotherapy is to reduce side effects.

Sternum—the flat bone that connects the clavicles and the first seven pairs of ribs; the breastbone.

Thymus Gland—a gland located in the chest behind the sternum that is involved in the development of the immune system.

White Count—the amount of white blood cells in the blood which protects the body against infection.

Resources

Resources

Informational Sources

www.breastcancer.org
A website devoted to providing medical information about breast cancer.

www.cancer.org
The American Cancer Society: the nationwide community-based voluntary health organization dedicated to eliminating cancer as a major health problem by preventing cancer, saving lives, and diminishing suffering from cancer through research, education, advocacy, and service.

1-800-ACS-2345

www.webmd.com
WebMD: a website for informational purposes only concerning a wide variety of health issues. It is not intended to be a substitute for professional medical advice, diagnosis, or treatment.

Treatment Centers

www.mayoclinic.com
The Mayo Clinic: empowers people to manage their health.

www.mdanderson.org
MDAnderson: working to eliminate cancer through integrated programs in cancer treatment, clinical trials, education programs and cancer prevention.

MDAnderson
1515 Holcombe Blvd
Houston, TX 77030
1-800-392-1611

www.stjudes.org
St. Jude Children's Research Hospital: one of the world's premier centers for research and treatment of catastrophic diseases in children, primarily pediatric cancers. The mission of St. Jude Children's Research Hospital is to advance cures, and means of prevention, for pediatric catastrophic diseases through research and treatment.

> St. Jude Children's Research Hospital
> 332 N. Lauderdale
> Memphis, TN 38105
> 1-866-278-5833

www.westclinic.com
The West Clinic: "A World-Class Center of Excellence for Oncology, Hematology, Radiology, and other Advanced Medical Care."

> East Memphis
> 100 N. Humphreys Blvd.
> Memphis, TN 38120
> 1-800-225-9971

Hair Helps

www.hatswithhair.com
Hats with Hair: specially designed partial wigs that combine hair with scarves, turbans, and hats. You can use your own hair. They also accept hair donations.

> Hip Hats with Hair
> by Fashion with Compassion
> 108 W. Adalee St.
> Tampa, FL 33603

www.locksoflove.com
Locks of Love: a public non-profit organization that provides hairpieces to financially disadvantaged children under age 18 suffering from long-term medical hair loss from any diagnosis.

> Locks of Love
> 2925 10th Ave. N
> Suite 102
> Lake Worth, FL 33461
> 1-888-896-1588

978-0-595-46623-8
0-595-46623-0

Printed in the United States
100642LV00002B/241-258/A